A STUDY OF COINS

A STUDY OF COINS

O. N. Singh & D. P. Sharma

Kaveri Books
New Delhi-110002

First Published in 2011
ISBN 978-81-7479-111-5

Published by
Kaveri Books
4832/24, Ansari Road
New Delhi - 110 002 (India)
Tel.: 011-2328 8140, 2324 5799,
Fax: 011-2328 8140
E-mail: kaveribooks@vsnl.com,
kaveribooks@gmail.com
Website: www.kaveribooks.com

Laser Typesetting by : Deep Graphics, Delhi

Printed at : Salasar Imaging Systems, Delhi-110 052

PRINTED IN INDIA

Dedicated to
Our Guru Dr. P.L. Gupta
(24.12.1914-29.07.2001)

Preface

Ancient South Asian coinages have a very long and varied historical tradition providing a rich source of information. Its value as a record of political and economic changes is enhanced by its narrative and aesthetic impact reflecting the cultural developments of different periods from 7th B.C. and regions. In fabric and execution South Asian coins show a remarkable skill and interesting techniques.

Ancient South Asian coinage begins with a uniform currency in silver and copper, known as the Punch-marked coins, found all over India. Issued between the 7th century B.C. and 1st century A.D. by merchant guilds and a few ruling families. It was mainly a trade currency belonging to a period of intensive trade activity and urban development. Trade also brought into India towards the close of this period, Roman coins in gold and silver, those of the emperors, Augustus and Tiberius being most common. South India has a concentration of Roman coin finds, especially along the trade routes and coastal areas (in Karnataka, Tamilnadu, Kerala and Andhra).

To the same period belong a series of local and regional coins viz., uninscribed cast copper coins and inscribed cast coins of the Janapadas i.e. monarchical and republican states of North India. These early indigenous issues starting from Punch-marked coins bore symbols of unknown import, perhaps drawn from tribal and popular cults, gradually giving place to those of the Buddhist and Brahmancial religions.

Regular dynastic coin issues begin with those of the foreign conquerors of west Asia Greek between the 2nd century B.C. and 2nd century A.D. viz. the Indo-Greeks, the Saka-Pahlavas and the Kushans. Hellenistic traditions characterize the silver coins of the Indo-Greeks, with Greek gods and goddesses figuring prominently, apart from the portraits of the issuers. These coins with their Greek legends are historically significant for the history of the Indo-Greeks has been reconstructed almost entirely on their evidence. The Saka coinages of the western Kshatrapas are perhaps the earliest dated coins, the dates being given in the Saka era of A.D.78, popular in Indian tradition of dating to this day.

It is with the Kushans that a variety of interesting features emerge in Indian coinage. While portraiture is common to all the 'foreign' issues and the early indigenous issues inspired by them, the Kushana gold coins introduce us to a series of new concepts, attributing divinity to royalty, iconographic forms drawn from Greek, Mesopotamian, Zorastrian and Indian mythology, Siva, Buddha and Kartikeya being the major Indian deities portrayed on them. The Kushana gold coins were undoubtedly the prototypes of the subsequent indigenous issues, especially those of the Guptas. However, for sheer variety, aesthetic sensitivity and rich narrative content, the Gupta gold coins remain unsurpassed by any other coinage of Ancient India.

Gupta coinage (320-578 A.D.) begins a process of indigenization, Greek and West Asian deities replaced by Indian divinities and Greek legends by Kharosthi & Brahmi. Apart from legitimizing dynastic succession Gupta gold coins commemorate significant socio-political events, like marriage alliances (king-and-queen type of coin of (Chandragupta I) and artistic and personal accomplishments of royal members (Lyrist, Archer, Horseman, Lion-slayer etc.) more significant are the iconographic representation of Puranic deities indicating the religious predilections of the Gupta rulers and the grandiose royal titles and epithets as coin legends in versified Sanskrit. Indeed the Gupta coinage reflects the classical art and literary idiom of the period. Gupta silver coins represent one of the few dynastic issues in silver.

Post-Gupta coinage (578-12th centuries A.D.), is represented by a monotonous and aesthetically less interesting series of dynastic issues including those of Harsha (7th centuries A.D) and early medieval Rajputs (9th-12th centuries A.D).

Ancient South Indian coinage of the early period belongs to a different tradition, remarkably conservative. The only exception is that of the Satavahanas (1st-2nd centuries A.D.) whose coins with portraits and bilingual legends were inspired by the Kshatrapa types. On the rest of the South Indian coin issues, the symbols are confined to dynastic crests such as the boar (Chalukya), bull (Pallava), tiger (Chola), fish (Pandya), bow and arrow (Chera) and lion (Hoysala) etc. Coin legends refer to names or titles of the issuer in local scripts and languages. Decorative features are rare and divinities are almost absent till the medieval Vijayanagar period (14th – 16th centuries A.D).

Among the foreign coins found in South India, mention must be made of the Chinese and Arab coins, which found their way into this region during periods of intensive trade i.e. beginning of Christian era and between 9th and 12th centuries A.D.

Medieval Indian coinage, represented by the Arab, Sultanate and Mughal coins, is dominated by Islamic traditions. Religious formulae such as the kalima (Islamic creed) the name of the Caliphas as spiritual heads. Quranic verses in beautiful calligraphy as coin legends are characteristic of all the issues, although deviations from this practice are not unknown.

Indigenous elements also have not been ignored. They are incorporated in various forms from the time of Mahmud Ghazni (10th-11th centuries A.D.) whose coins bear legends both in the Arabic Kufic and Sanskrit-Nagari scripts. Goddess Laxmi was featured on the coins of Muhammad Ghori.

The North Deccan gold which filled the coffers of the Khaljis, was turned into an interesting series of coins of Alau-d-din Khalji with titles like 'Sikander-al-Sani'. But it is Muhammad bin Tughluq who is known to history as an innovator and reformer of currency. His currency is economically significant.

Originality and innovative skill characterize the Mughal coinage, which ranks among the greatest currencies of the world. Jahangir in his Tuzuk-I-Jahangiri speaks with justifiable pride of the innovations he made in his coinage. The zodiacal signs, portraits and literary verses in excellent calligraphy that he introduced on his coins were preceded by the Ilahi coins of Akbar, which commemorate the religious ideals the emperor cherished. In contrast, Aurangzeb,s omission of the Kalima on his coins is believed to be an indication of his firm devotion to Islam, as it was done in order not to defile the creed.

Mint names with honorific prefixes like 'Dar al-Khilafat Shahjahanabad' (Delhi) and dates of issue are the other characteristic features of Mughal coinage. It is however, to Sher Shah Suri (A.D.1540-45), whose reign was an interlude in Mughal history, goes the credit of standardization of currency the silver coins of a specific weight i.e. tola (178 grains) –which formed the basis of all the subsequent silver issues leading to the emergence of the modern rupee.

The Vijaynagar contemporaries of the Delhi Sultanate and Mughals were the only Hindu dynasty whose currency presents a rare example of a standarised issue which later provided a model for the European and English trading companies. Particularly significant are the Vijayanagar coins with the deity of Tirupati i.e. Venkatesvara represented either singly or with his two consorts inspiring 'Single Swami' pagodas of the Dutch and French and the 'Three Swami' Pagodas of the English East Indian Company.

Modern Indian coinage is represented by the issues of European and English trading companies and the Indian states under British rule. The coins of the Indian states continue Mughal tradition with some deviations such as the introduction of local rulers' names till they were finally absorbed into the single currency system introduced by the British after 1857. Exceptions to this are a few states such as the Travancore, Hyderabad etc. Notable among the Indian state issues are those of the Mysore Sultans (A.D.1772-1799). Haider Ali issued 'Pagodas' depicting Hidnu deities while Tipu Sultan, is known for his variety of gold coins incorporating typical Islamic and Hindu features. His gold coins were named after the orthodox Caliphs, his silver coins after the twelve Imams and copper after astronomical phenomena.

The European and English trading companies (17th-19th centuries A.D), brought with them their respective currencies such as the Dutch Stuiver, Venetian Ducat, Portuguese Cruzado and English Angelina and Carolina. However, imitation of local coins was a common practice among the trading companies with Vijayanagar coins providing well known prototypes. The adoption of the Mughal rupee by the trading companies and

British rulers of India marked the end of independent currency systems and the beginning of a uniform currency in India.

The coinage of independent India has undergone a number of changes. The three main factors necessitating the changes have been, chronologically, (1) advent of independence from foreign rule (2) Introduction of the metric system, and (3) the need felt from time to time to obviate the possibility of the metallic value of coins rising beyond the face value.

We are indebted to Dr. K.K. Chakravarty Chancellor NUEPA, New Delhi, Prof. D.P. Singh, V.C. B.H.U, Prof. C.D. Singh V.C. IGNTU Amearkantak, Prof. Upender Singh, Prof. Nayanjot Lahri, Prof. V.D. Mishra, Prof. S.R. Dubey, HOD, A.I.H.C. & Arch., and Dr. Savita Sharma for encouraging us in bringing out this publication. Photographs used here are courtesy of National Museum, New Delhi, Bharat Kala Bhavan, BHU Varanasi, and Prof. Upender Singh.

Authors are thankful to Mr. Rakesh Goel of Kaveri Books, New Delhi for publishing this book within short period. The photography work was done by Mr. Ajit Kumar Choudhary & computer typing was done by Mr. Bahadur Kannujya. Authors are also thankful to all the Librarian & Library staff like Mr. S.B. Singh of Bharat Kala Bhavan, BHU and our research scholars & students like Dr. Priyanka Singh, Sushil Kr. Singh, Sujeet Kr. Singh, Vinay Kr. Singh, Samvedna Singh.etc

Dr. O. N. Singh
Dr. D.P. Sharma

Contents

List of Plates

Chapter 2: Tribals Coins of Ancient India

Chapter 3: Indo-Greek Coins

Chapter 7: Gupta Coins

List of Maps

Introduction

Currency and coinage are more specific terms. Currency is a medium of exchange backed by an issuing authority, one that can be used to immediately discharge any kind of financial obligation. Coinage is metal currency. It has a definite size, shape and weight standard, and bears the stamp of an issuing authority. The main message bearing side of a coin is known as the obverse and the other side the reverse. In the world context, the earliest coins appear in Lybia in West Asia in were made of electrum, a natural alloy of gold and silver. Harappan disc shaped gold bead is the oldest coin in India.

Mint towns can be identified by noting sites where large numbers of coin moulds have been found. An analysis of coin dies can help identify the number and sequence of issues and estimates of the volume of coins produced by these dies can be made by extrapolation. Stone age people had neither currency nor coinage and conducted exchange via barter. Chalcolithic cultures too conducted trade without the use of coins. They also did exchange via barter the Harappans 2700-1900 B.C. for instance, had a very extensive trade network based on barter. Some scholar suggested copper tablet disc shaped gold beads discovered from Mohenjodaro and Mandi were used coins but these seem to take in trade 2500-1900 B.C. The Rigveda text composed 2000-1500 B.C. mentions words such as *nishka* and *nishka-griva* (gold ornaments), and *hiranya-pinda* (gold globules), but these cannot be understood as coins Gold ornament nishka griva was reported from *Monds*. Later Vedic texts which were composed between 1500-1000 B.C. use terms such as *nishka, suvarna, shatamana,* and *pada*. These may have been metal pieces of definite weight, not necessarily full-fledged coins. Disc shaped bead and copper tablet of Harappan are nishka (Rigveda event is contemporary of Early Harappan 3500-2800 B.C.)

The earliest definite literary and archaeological evidences of coinage in the Indian subcontinent dates from the 7th -6th centuries BCE in context of the emergence of states, urbanization, and expanding trade. The basic unit of Indian coin weight systems was a red-and-black seed of the *gunja* berry (*Abrus precatorius*) known as the *raktika, ratti*, or *rati*. The advent of coinage did not mean the disappearance of barter- both co-existed for a very long time.

The oldest coins found in the subcontinent are punch-marked coins, made mostly of silver, some of copper 700-600 B.C. They are usually rectangular, sometimes square or round. The blanks for making these coins were generally cut from a metal sheet or made from flattened metal globules. The symbol were then hammered on separately, using dies or punches.

The punch-marked coins of northern India can be divided into four series on the basis of their weight, the number and nature of punch marks, and their area of circulation- the Taxila-Gandhara type of the north-west a heavy weight standard and a single punch type; the Kosala type of the middle Ganga valley, with a heavy weight standard and multiple punch marks; the Avanti type of western India, with a light weight standard and single punch mark; and the Magadhan type with a light weight standard and multiple punches.

Symbols on these coins include geometric designs, plants, animals, the sun, wheel, mountain, tree (including tree-in-railing), branches and human figures. Some symbols may have had a religious or political importance, but their precise significance is not always certain. The coins often have primary and secondary punch marks.

Uninscribed cast coins made of copper of alloys of copper appeared soon after the punch-marked coins, which seem to have been issued in the late 3rd of early 2nd century BCE. These coins were made by melting metal and pouring it into clay or metal moulds. Clay moulds have in fact been found at many sites and a bronze mould was found at Eran in Central India.

Other early Indian coin types include uninscribed die-struck coins, mostly in copper, rarely in silver. The symbols, some similar to those on the punch-marked coins, were struck onto coin blanks with metal dies that were carefully carved with the required designs. The minting of such coins may have begun in about the 4th century BCE and they have been found in large number at sites such as Taxila and Ujjain.

The die-struck Indo-Greek coins of the 2nd/1st century BCE. These are very well-executed, usually round (a few are square or rectangular) and mostly in silver (a few are in copper, billon [a silver-copper alloy] nickel, and lead). They bear the name and portrait of the issuing ruler on the obverse. Coins of Menander and Strato I show them slowly aging from teenagers to old men, indicating their long reigns. Coins issued jointly by kings reflect the practice of conjoint rule. The coins of these kings also have certain symbols referred to monograms by numismatists, the precise significance of which is not certain.

27 BC, the traditional date of the beginning of the Roman Empire, saw no radical change in the coinage. Late Imperatorial issues were very much like the first coins of

Caesar Augustus as emperor. The assumption of the title ***Augustus*** (revered one) merely confirmed the position that Octavian had held since the defeat of Antony at Actium in 31 B.C. Rulers following Augustus would also assume this title as the identifying mark of the Emperor. Our examples below will skim the surface of Roman ***Imperial*** coins from the beginning of the Empire until the death of Commodus in the late 2nd century A.D. Later pages will extend this date to the end of the Empire. Most of the significant terms have been covered on the earlier pages of this series. These will be reinforced and joined by a few more. So vast a subject can hardly be covered with so small a page but the beginning student will be able to derive from these samples a general overview of Roman Imperial coins.

The Kushanas (50 B.C. – 3rd C. A.D.) were the first dynasty of the subcontinent to mint large quantities of gold coins; their silver coins are rare. Vima Takto & Vima Kadphises first issued gold coins during early 1st C. A.D. They also issued many copper coins of low denominational value, which indicates the increasing spread of the money economy. Deccan, the punch mark coinage was followed by the copper and silver coins of the Satavahana kings, Rulers of this dynasty also issued coins of small denominational value made of lead and potin. Most Satavahana coins were die-struck, but there are some cast coins, and a combination of techniques was also used. The legends were generally in the Prakrit language and Brahmi script. However, the portrait coins (mostly in silver, but also in lead) use a Dravidian language and Brahmi script.

There was greater demand for silver currency in the western Deccan, prehaps due to commercial reasons. The Kshatarapa ruler Nahapana introduced a silver currency in the Nashik area. Roman gold coins also followed into peninsular India in large quantities in the early centuries CE and may have been used as a medium of exchange for large-scale transactions or as currency reserves and capital deposits. Locally made imitations of Roman gold coins have also been found.

Some of the punch-marked coins found in various parts of South India have been identifies as dynastic issues on the basis of their symbols. For example, coins found in a hoard at Bodinaikkanur near Madurai had a double carp fish- the symbol of the Pandya kings. Coins with the legend *valuti* have been assigned to the Pandyas. Silver coins with the portrait of a *Chera* king and the legend *Makkatai* have been found in the Krishna river bed near *Karur*.

The imperial Gupta kings issued well-executed die-struck gold coins with metrical legends in Sanskrit. Known as *dinaras*, these coins have been mostly found in north India. The obverse depicts the reigning king in various poses, usually martial ones, but there are interesting instances of coins of Samudragupta and Kumaragupta I showing them playing the *vina* (a stringed instrument). The reverse of the Gupta coins have religious symbols indicating the kings' religious affiliations. There was a decline in the metallic purity of gold coins in the later part of Skandagupta's reign. The Guptas also issued silver coins, but their copper coins are rare.

The die-sinkers of Chandragupta II (circa AD 375-413) and his son Kumaragupta I were given the task of applying this ancient motif in their designs. On their coins of the parasol type the majestic king stands to the left in full glory, shielded by his white parasol held by an attendant. He offers oblations on an altar as a token of his devotion to the gods. Depending on the die design the king may appear with or without a halo. His clothes vary as well, but Chandragupta always wears a long sword, one of the weapons of the ancient Indian noble warrior. The most obvious symbol for the might of a *chakravartin* is the wheel. It is also the attribute par excellence of Vishnu, the divine model for the Gupta king. The mint masters of Chandragupta II skilfully combined the two notions in the *chakravikrama* type. On these rare coins the invincible *chakrapurusha,* the personified wheel, offers three small round objects to a princely figure on his left, representing chandragupta. The three pellets have been explained as symbolizing authority (*prabhu-shakti*), energy (*utsaha-shakti*), and counsel (*mantra-shakti*), which are essential conditions for successful rule. The personified wheel has been described as resting his left hand on a mace, but it may be a conch or a small vessel instead. He wears a waist-cloth, a long sash, and probably a low crown or a diadem.

The nimbate king wears similar clothes and ornaments (but no sash). His belt secures a long dagger. With his right hand chandragupta accepts the gift from the *chakrapurusha*. His left hand rests on the hilt of his sword. Together the *chakrapurusha* and the king aptly illustrate the epithet *chakravikrama*, "in valour (or 'in course') as the wheel" inscribed on the reverse.

Majestic leisure may be a fitting description of the theme illustrated by chandragupta II portrayed on a low seat with a high, decorated backrest. He sits with either once or both feet drawn up on his seat, and lifts a lotus flower to his face as if trying to catch its lovely fragrance. In some die designs he has been given a halo. Usually his seat is called a couch, and this coin type has been named after it. However, it is not significantly different from other seats customarily described as thrones. Whether couch or throne, in this design the seat evidently serves as an emblem of Chandragupta's royal status.

Samundragupta displays a more erudite form of royal leisure on his coins of the lyrist type, which were also issued by Kumaragupta I. In this highly artistic design the bare-chested king sits cross-legged to left on a low seat with a high, decorated backrest. His right foot rests on a footstool.

These texts explain that the performer of the horse sacrifice is without *shri* during the year-long absence of the horse. Apparently the design does not refer specifically to the horse sacrifice, but to the king's *shri*. Samudragupta is shown playing an instrument which, according to the *Shatapatha Brahmana*, symbolizes royal fortune.

This king and queen type has frequently been described as illustrating and commemorating the marriage itself, but the scene does not show a recognizable rite from that ceremony. Chandragupta I and his queen, usually both nimbate, stand facing each other. Each has been identified by his or her name. The king rests his left hand on a scepter topped by a crescent. With his right hand he offers a ring or a scarf to Kumaradevi.

Quite exceptionally the reverse legend does not give any royal's name or epithet, but mentions the Lichchhavis instead. The Allahabad Pillar inscription also specifically alludes to Samudragupta's descent from the Lichchhavis ("*Lichchhavidauhitrasya*", of the son of the daughter of [the] Lichchhavi'). Evidently, Samudragupta was proud of this ancestry and his decision to mentions the Lichchhavis on a coin portraying his Lichchhavi mother and his Gupta father may have been instigated by the same pride.

Samudragupta's motive for circulating coins with the images of his parents, Chandragupta I (*circa* AD 319-350) and Kumaradevi. She was a princess of the Lichchhavi tribe from Vaishali, in Bihar. By their marriage the Gupta principality was fused with the Lichchhavi territory into a much more powerful territorial nucleus for the Gupta expansion to come.

Kumaragupta I's king and queen coins show a nimbate, sword-bearing king identified by his name as Kumara (gupta) himself, offering a flower to the lady at his side, whose name is not visible on the flan. A number of base metal alloy coin series were issued by dynasties in early medieval times. In the plain, Billon coins circulated in the Gurjara-Pratihara kingdom, while other coin types circulated in Rajputana and Gujarat. Copper coins were minted by the Arab governors of Sindh between the mid-8th to mid -9th centuries.

In the western Deccan, some early medieval coin types have been tentatively identified with the Chalukyas of Badami. Although gold and silver coins found in the Andhra region have been attributed to the early eastern Chalukyas. Coins issued by the Kadambas of Goa (11th – 12th centuries) have been identified, and a few gold coins have been attributed to the Shilaharas of the western Deccan (11th century).

In the far south, coins with lion and bull motifs, some inscribed with titles, have been associated with the Pallavas. Gold coins found at Kavilayada valli in the Nellore district of Andhra Pradesh have the motifs of the tiger, bow, and some indistinct marks. The obverse has the Tamil legend sung which seems to be a short form of *sungandavirttarulina* (abolisher of tolls), one of the titles of the Chola king kulottunga. In many parts of early medieval India, cowries continued to be used as money along with coins. At Sohepur in Orissa, 25,000 cowries were found along with 27 Kalachuri coins. At Bhaundri village in Lucknow, 54 Pratihara coins were found along with 9,834 cowries. The market value of cowries fluctuated, depending on demand and supply.

The wide distribution of Kushana coins indicates the flourishing trade of the period. The ship on certain Satavahana coins reflects the importance of maritime trade in the Deccan during this period. Roman coins found in various part of India provide information on Indo-Roman trade.

All the coin legends were in the Prakrit language and proclaimed Nahapana as the Kshatrapa of the Kshaharata house. Gautamiputra Satakarni counter-struck Nahapana's coins with his own symbols. Another interesting example of counter-striking comes from certain coins issued by Nahapana with counter-strikes by an otherwise unknown Satavahana king named Shiva Satakami. The depiction of deities on coins provides information about the personal religious preferences of kings, royal religious policy, and the history of religious cults. For instance, representations of Balarama and Krishna appear on 2nd century BCE coins of the Indo-Greek king Agathocles at AI-Khanoum (in Afghanistan).

CHAPTER-1

Early Coins of India

In Vedic times people used gold for various purpose such as for making ornaments and subsequently for their currency and money in order to do trade and commerce. Gold was found in abundance and was still popular in other parts of India due to its texture, quality and purity.

Herodotus known as the Father of History tells us that 300 talents of gold dust was annually paid as a periodical payment by the conquered state to the treasury of the Achaemenid Empire during 518 B.C. to 350 B.C. due to the inclusion of Indian province in it. No gold coins are known in India till this date before the advent of the Indo-Bactrians in the second-first centuries B.C.

The coins are still playing an important role in today's human life in relation to ancient times, but how they were manufactured in the early period on a large scale is a big question and is not found in the still existing Indian literature. However in the state of Chandragupta Maurya, his sagacious minister Kautilya better known as Chanakya has incidentally gave the counterfeiters of coins (Kuta-rupakaraka) in his Arthashastra, the book on statecraft compiled in the fourth century BC. In this book, he has mentioned a list of objects that were used in the manufacture of coins.

In this long manufacturing process of coins it shows that first of all metal was melted crucibles (mūsha) and cleaned with alkalis (substance which forms salt with acid): then the metal was beaten into sheets on an anvil (adhikarni) with a hammer (mushtika) and then cut into pieces with clippers (sandānsa) and at last they were suppressed with dies or purchase which contains symbols (bimba-tanka). Even today in all over the world in order to save the automatic mechanical devices the same process is used in mints for the manufacture of coins.

The actual Indian coins of the early period exhibits that they were cut and designed in such a way to adjust them into proper weight. The early period coins were found in various geometrical forms like oval, round and elliptical. At internals in order to give a desired shape, metal in the appropriate weight of coin was melted and poured on to the earth or on some level surface to take its shape.

The pellets were also made from the molten metal and flattened. The flan which was made imprint with the help of bold punches bearing devices on one side of the coins. As a result these ancient coins bear the stamps of one to five punches, unlike today's coins. By using this technique these coins are known as punch-marked coins amongst historians and numismatists.

Punch-marked coins may be defined as those ancient coins which were made by punching symbols or signs on them using punching devices. They are without any definite shape. These coins may be long, circular pentagonal or hexagonal. There were no inscriptions to be found on the punching devices of the early Indian coins rather these devices found in various forms and shapes viz., various forms of hills, trees, human figures, animals, birds, floral, various geometrical designs or patterns as wells as religious symbols. These devices were used with some particular system and as a result the punching devices of these early coins can be found into several unlimited varieties.

The symbols on these coins were related to a particular region or to a particular class or group. In this way, one can separate the coins of one area from those of another viz., state and period. The front part of a coin is known as *obverse* and the other side is called *reverse*. On the ancient coins the marks were originally stamped on the obverse or the front side whereas the reverse side remained blank. In course of time, the back part or side was also used to impress some minute marks on it while they were in circulation.

The coins having the same symbol or group of symbols on the obverse may be see either to be blank on the reverse or with some minute marks punched there on. The marks may be only one or two and at a time even ten or twelve.

The symbols on punch-marked coins have been divided into the following categories viz., simple symbols, animals, birds, river, and human figures. The coins which were in longer circulation got more stamps than these which were in shorter circulation due to which some of the marks are generally lightly punched, look new whereas others appear quite worn out on the same coin. To certify the bonafides of the coins in respect of their weight and metal the marks are of the shroffs, bankers or money tests and were affixed in all probability. These early silver punch-marked coins I have been found in quite large amount scattered all over the country. The earliest of them which were found in a particular area or locality were issued by the *janapada* and *mahajanapadas* (small and big states) which existed after the Bharat war (c. 11 century) when Magadha empire rose in the fifty century B.C. these were became part of it which spread over the whole country by the end of the fourth century B.C.

The states which issued these coins are : Sūrasena (modern Braj, the region around Mathura), Uttar Panchala (the region of Rohilkhand) Dakshina Paṃchāla (the doab area stretching from the Ganga to the Chambal), Vatsa (the region south of the Ganga, extending upto Avanti or Ujjain), Kunāla (modern Gonda-Bahraich districts), Kosala (the area bounded by the Gomti on the west, Sarpikā-modern Sai on the south Sadānera - modem Gandak on the east and the Nepal hills on the north, Kashi (the region around Varanasi including parts of the districts of Jaunpur, Ghazipur and Mirzapur), Malla (districts of Deoria and its surroundings), Magadha (it included the area bounded by the Ganga on the north and Son on the west, dense forest covered the plateau of Chhota Nagpur to the south and Bhagalpur region to the east), Vanga (Bengal), Kalinga (the coastal area from Vaitarni in Orissa to the borders of Andhra, extending in the west into the hilly forests to Amarkantak, Madhya Pradesh, Andhra (the delta of the Govadari and the Krishna), Aśmaka (the south of Godavari in Maharashtra), Mulaka (neighboring state of Aśmaka including Hyderabad) Surashtra (the Kathiawar region) and Gandhara (the north western region on the border of Afghanistan.

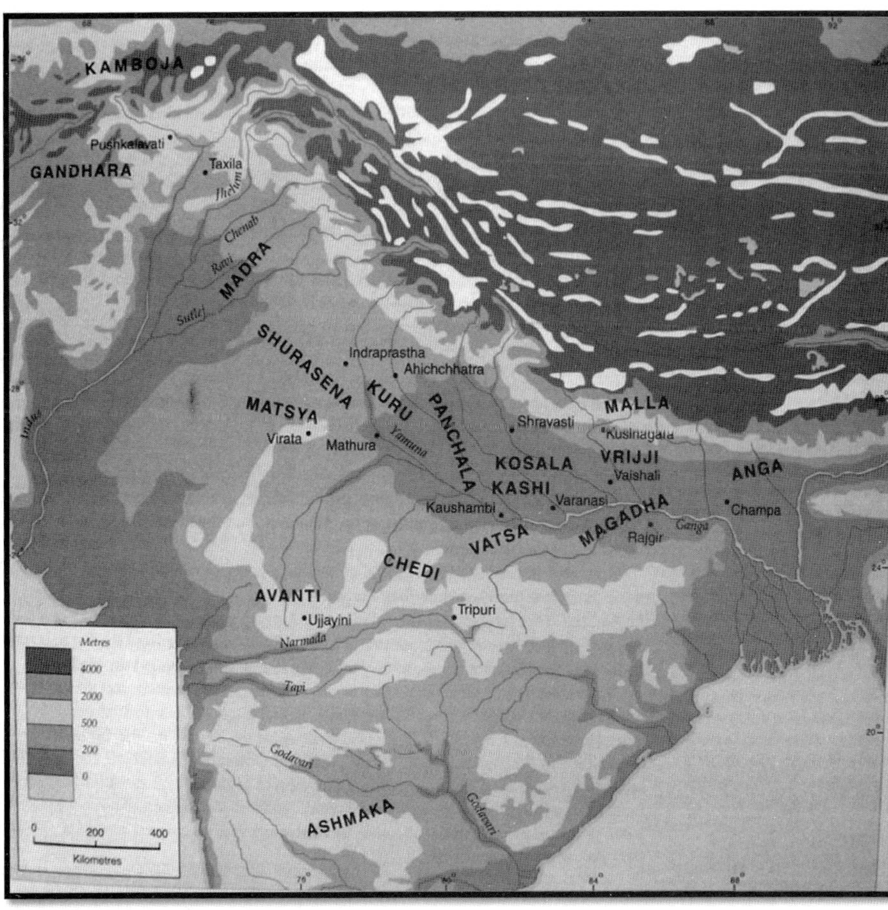

Map 1: Map of 16 Mahajanpadas after Upender Singh

During the Brahmana and Upanishad period i.e. circa eight century B.C., some or probably all of these states might have been using metal as a currency and money for various purposes. Thereafter with the passage of time the idea of coins came into existence in some of the states. But who was its initiator, from which date it were the first earliest coins we have nothing yet to hint. Rather it is only said that these coins came into existence before fifth century B.C. and gradually disappeared when the Magadha empire expanded by the end of the fourth century B.C. The coins of all these states were differ from each other particularly in their weight, quality of metal, execution, structure and symbology. The states which used only one symbol on their coins and their symbols differed from each other in their shape and execution are Sūrasena, Uttar Paṃchāla, Dakshina Paṃchāla, Kunāla, Surāshtra and Aśmaka.

The coins of these excluding Aśmaka and Kunāla are pieces cut from metal sheets and stamped subsequently whereas the coins of Aśmaka and Kunāla were produced by the pouring out molten metal on a smooth level surface got stamped when the metal was still soft.

The Aśmaka coins are thick, circular or oval in shape and slightly scyphate. The symbol which is made in bold relief with a deep circular incuse which symbol is simple, in which two small pulleys joint to a bigger pulley with two separate belts. They may, be found in three distinct weights- 99 to 108 grains, 45 to 58 grains and 21 to 23 grains respectively.

On the other hand, the Kunāla coins are thick dumpy pieces; their shape is irregular and linear and the symbol on them is stamped in bold relief with a deep circular incuse. Their weight varies from 105 and 50 grains.

Next came the coins of Surāshtra which are thin small pieces of 15 grains approximately. Almost the full die appears on them, only the sides are slightly out of flan. The symbol on it represents a bull surrounded by several minute symbols.

The coins of Sūrasena, Uttar Pānchāla and Dakshina Pānchāla are found of the weight standard of 25 grains. Besides this, in execution and symbology, the coins of Sūrasena and Uttar Pānchāla are similar. The main features are : Both are tiny thick pieces with only a portion of the punch or die impressed. The symbols found on the Uttar Paṃchala coins were fish, bull, elephant with or without a rider; whereas Sūrsena have a cat or a lion- like animal placed over two inverted semi-circles and Taurine, suggestive of a hill. The reverse of the coins of both the states remained blank.

The coins of Dakshina Panchala are different from the coins of Surasena and Uttar Panchala. They may be found in more than hundred varieties due to the symbol punched on them. The symbol punched on them are round, composed of dots, solid and hollow circles, lines, squares, taurine and many more; these components are arranged variously in a systematic manner to form the symbols. But on these coins no symbol seen in its full form because the punches being bigger than the flans. On the other hand, the back part or the reverse of the coins is stamped with minute marks, punched with such heavy striking which appears blurred because the obverse symbols smashed between the blows of the hammer and the resistance of the anvil.

The early silver punch-marked coins of Gandhara are a concave long bar with a singular shape. The coins were about 0.1 mek.sim of inch to 1.75¾ in length and 0.4¾ in width. The bar appear to be strips cut from oblong ingots. Thickness remaining the same but the length of the coins is determined by the width of the ingots. The strips were, therefore, cut into a width which combined with the other two dimensions, gave the required weight to the coins. After being cut, the corners of the bars were chiseled and some time the obverse sides so that they can adjusts more correctly to the weight. At each end of the bar, a common symbol was punched on them twice and the coins on a wooden anvil were struck while they were hot. As a result the coins appeared hollow. The dies that used for punching the coins were substantially wider than the pieces due to which the full symbol is rarely seen on the coins. The symbol is a circular design composed of a six tridents and a pole radiating from a central circle when the coin is new it is found of 183 grains but in general their weight ranges between 150 to 183 grains. Sometimes on the concave side, some minute punches are also noticed as a test marks. Gandhara covered the area of the north western region on the border of Afghanistan which was ruled by the Persians from the end of the sixth to the middle of the fourth century B.C. The coins which were found were based on the weight standard of the Persian siglos and represented double sigloi. Coins of smaller denominations weighting 90, 80, 43, 20 and 7 grains are also known as having been used by this state. They are found in a cup shaped, irregular pieces with only one punch of the same symbol which is also found on the bigger ones.

Vanga coins are basically thin, rectangular pieces about half an-inch and their weight between 50-52 grains they have three distinct symbols:

(a) A single-decked ship; (b) a wheel and

(c) A six-armed symbol consisting of six arrows placed around a double circle.

The coins of Vatsa, Kosala, Kasi, Magdha, Kalinga and Andhra are thin in fabric whereas the coins of Malla and Mūlaka are thick and dumpy. The coins of all these states bearing four symbols found in three distinct orientations:

(i) Two symbols in two pairs constitute the four symbols. Each pair facing inwards towards each other.

(ii) One pair of one symbol and two odd symbols; i.e. three symbols constitute the group of four symbols;

(iii) Four different symbols constitute the group.

These all three forms are found on the coins of Magadha and Vatsa; Kāśi issued their coins in only two forms; Mūlaka in the second form; Andhra in the second and third forms; whereas the coins of Kosala, Malla and Kalinga have only the symbols of the third form. These arrangements of the symbols appear to have evolved from one into the other.

Now we shall discuss the main features of the coins of these states. First of all we will take into account the coins of Vatsa which are broad, thin pieces of about an inch in size and have a roundish shape. The symbols which are found on them are animal figures, six- armed symbols various geometrical patterns, a scorpion - like object associated with other marks. The latter symbol is most conspicuous and the coins weight about 50 to 54 grains.

The earliest coins of Kosala are broad, thin rounded pieces. The obverse side appeared battered due to the heavy minute punchings on the reverse side of the coins. The later coins are of a medium-thick fabric with a minute symbols on the reverse without any effect on the obverse. The symbols on these coins are mostly geometrical shapes, elephant, bull, hare and trees of various forms are seen. The most conspicuous symbol on these coins is composed of three S- like objects placed around a small pellet. The coins generally found of about 42 grains only. We can compared the coins of Kashi with that of Vatsa and early Kosala coins due to their thin and elliptical fabric; but these coins appear a little saucer-like because of symbols which were punched on them. On these coins one pair of symbols is smaller in size than the other. The symbols are composed of a complex of whorls, consisting of four arms hazing several curved branches. We can also found lotus patterns symbols and the weight of the coins of about 75 grains.

The coins of Andhra state are small in size, thin pieces of irregular shape. The symbols are neatly punched of about 20 grains. The most common symbol which is found on the coins is an elephant facing left or right. Other symbols include geometrical patterns or designs made by circles, dots, curved lines, taurines and many conventionalised forms of trees. The bull is also occasionally found. Kalingas coins are also very similar to the Andhra coins in their fabric and weight and they follow one of its varieties for their symbols.

The coin of Mūlaka kingdom is a thick, small in size with a round shape of 65 grains; out of the four symbols, two are the repetition of the same symbol. The symbol in a pair is a simple one, made of semi-oval lines; the other two odd symbols are (a) six knobbed rays around a circle appears like a sun, and (b) a duck-like bird flying over a hill.

We can study the Mall coins by grouping them into two distinct series. The coins of one series appear like dumphy ingots and weigh- 65 grains. They bear two symbols in which one is bigger than the other and are composed of simple lines. The coins of the second series are of two denominations. The coins of the higher denomination weight 48-50 grains and have four symbols on them and those of the lower denomination weight only 10-12 grains bear-only two symbols. Their symbols are simple geometrical patterns.

The Magadha coins can be labelled as (i) local coins that were issued in the reign of its Kingdom and (ii) during the period of its imperial expansion and are found all over the country. The 'local' Magadhan coins are grouped into three distinct series probably belonging to three series.

The coins of first series are found of two denominations in which the coins of higher denomination are thin, oval flat pieces, about one and a half inches in length and about one inch in width with two neat symbols punched on them in which the one symbol is smaller than the other; but both are lotus patterns, different in form. They found of 125 grains. The coins of the lower denomination have a small lotus symbol of about 3 grains only. The coins of the second series are about in four denominations. The coins of two higher denominations manufacture by rolling the molten metal flat in round elliptical in shape when the metal is still hot the impression appeared blurred on those pieces which were generally not become solid fully and are incomplete on those which were stamped when the metal had cooled.

The coins of the highest denomination bear four symbols. Some coins have two pairs of two symbols and two odd symbols. In both cases on pair of symbols is smaller in size the other two symbols. Lesser denomination coins have only one symbol on them and the weights of these two denominations are 92-97 grains and 46-49 grains respectively.

The coins of other two denominations of the second series are quite different particularly in their fabric. Their structure also differs from other coins made of thin sheets with a long circular ends in the case of the bigger coins whereas small circular ends in case of the smaller coins. On the bigger coins there were two symbols punched on them but the smaller ones with one symbol. By the pressure of the dies, the bigger coins look like a boat and the smaller ones like a pan (thali). The symbols on the obverse have risen up in relief and sunken down on the reverse; look like repousse work.

The weights of the coins of the two denominations are 13-16 grains and 7-8 grains respectively. The coins of all the four denominations, though made of two different fabrics, have a six- armed symbol but cannot impressed properly. The Rulers of the Bārhadratha dynasty with their capital at Girivraja i.e. Rajagriha issued these coins in their reign.

The local Magadha coins of the third series are thin, broad pieces, just like those of the Vatsa, Kosala and Kasi. They have four well-executed symbols with a weight of about 72 grains the four symbols are: (a) the sun with sixteen rays; (b) a six-armed symbol with three taurines and three ovals placed one after the other; (c) a bull facing left in a standing position and (d) a lion standing in left side. The last ruler of the Magadha kingdom issued the coins of this series. The Magadha had begun to develop into an empire during the reign of Ajatasatru.

During the Imperial period the coins that were issued were circulating throughout the country from the time of Ajatasatru down to the end of the Mauryan dynasty in the second century B.C. are of regular weight standard which was of 54 grains in approximate. The coins that are generally found during this period weighing between 50 to 52 grains and almost in fresh condition. These are basically pieces cut out from metal sheets and all are in conceivable shapes. Regarding size they are found as broad as 1.25" and as 0.4". In relation to size their thickness also varies between .02" and 1.25". The broad coins are thin and the small coins are thick.

In chronology the thin coins are the earliest and thick one are the latest. Each coins have fire symbols punched using five different punches. The symbols that are used on these coins are of different geometrical patterns ranging from simple to complex, human figures, animals such as bulls, elephant, a rhinoceros, a fish, a tortoise, a hare, a crocodile, the sun, trees and mountains in many conventional forms. More than 300 varieties of symbols may be recognized on them. The variety of symbols used on those coins are placed in a definite symbol or order, through which one can mark difference between them according to their symbol groups and can identify them in about 500 varieties. These varieties may be in turn can be classified into different groups and ultimately into six series. These six series of coins may be placed into a chronology on the basis of the fabric. The first and second series of coins are of a thin fabric whereas the next two series of coins of a medium fabric. It means that few coins of third series are found of a thin fabric and likewise a few coins of series four in a thick fabric. The coins of series five are mixture of both, medium and thick fabric. The last series i.e. six series of which the coins are exclusively of a thick fabric. As on earlier coins the minute symbols that to be found on the reverse side, in the same way these symbols are also described on the first four series of coins. The coins of series five are minute marks as well as a new type of mark, which is distinct from the earlier ones. The six series coins have a bold mark on them and these bold reverse symbols are always exclusive to a particular class or variety. Thus we arrive at the conclusion that the study of punch-marked coins of the imperial period is not an easy task and we can only said that each series of coins belongs to particular dynasty or a particular ruler; in some cases, they may also be identified as the issues of different mints.

But what actually the symbols that are punched on these coins mean has not yet been ascertained. They are as enigmatic as the Harappan script.

The issue of the silver punch marked coins but to halt in the second century B.C. for some time, but the coinage exerted a wide influence during the next four or five hundred years. During the Gupta period, no silver coin is known in Uttar Pradesh and Bihar. Only punch-marked coins of the Magadha Empire were in circulation. Through archaeological excavation they are found in various levels. Using the die-striking process, the shortage of these coins was replenished by reproducing these old coins.

Terracotta casting moulds for making the coins have been found at Mathura, Jhusi (Allahabad), Sisupalagarh (Orissa) and Kondapur (Andhra Pradesh) bronze matrix with the impression of a punch-marked coin has come to light from Eran (Madhya Pradesh).

In Kautilya's *Arthasastra* it is mentioned that silver coins of four denominations viz., pana ardha-pana (half pana) Pada (quarter pana) and ashta-bhaga or ardhapadika (one eight pana) were being issued from the Mauryan emperors mints. But only one denomination of weighing 50-52 grains are known throughout the Magadhan empire identified as pana, also known as Karashapana. However, in a number of hoards, a few coins have been found which merely pieces are cut from full coins. They suggest that full coins were cut into halves for the purpose of half denominations and were accepted as legal tender. This type of dichotomy is seen in some places in the later period also. Some minute coins, weighing 2 and 3 grains, made by flattening the metal globules with a symbol stamped on them look same to these which are found on the imperial panas are the only silver pieces that were used in transactions during this period. The minute coins that are found occasionally along with the Imperial panas were also known as mashaka i.e. one- sixteenth of a pana Kautilya also writes that during the period of Mauryas most likely reddish malleable metal i.e. copper was used for coins in place of silver. But copper punchmarked coins was rare and are most likely local issues, issued in the post-Mauryan period.

The regions where they have been found are Magadha-Anga, Ujjain-Vidisa, Mathura and Mewar (Rajasthan). But the copper coins that found were produced by casting from moulds which was totally different from the punch-marked technique were widely circulated in almost all parts of northern India in several varieties. The most common of them are small round coins with an elephant on the obverse and the three-arched hill on the reverse. Sometimes, two coins of this variety are found attached together with a small band of metal in between the two. Copper punch-marked coins were in circulation from the third century B.C. to the third century A.D. but their manufacture stopped during the first century B.C. It is not certain whether they are meant for circulation or they are mint breaks.

References

Agarwal, B. and Rai, S. Indian Punch Marked Coins, New Delhi,1994.

Allan, J. A Catalogue of the Coins in the British Museum: Coins of Ancient India, London,1936

Bhandarkar, D.R. The Annual Report of the Archaeological Survey of India, 1913-14

Cunningham, A. Coins of Ancient India, London, 1891

Dhawalikar, M.K. The Beginning of Coinage in India, Delhi, 1975

Goyal, S.R. The Coinage of Ancient India, Jodhpur, 1995

Gupta, P.L. Punch Marked Coins in the Andhra Pradesh Government Museum, Hyderabad, 1906

— Amravati Hoard of Silver Punch Marked Coins, Andhra Pradesh, 1963

— Bibliography of the Hoard of the Punch Marked Coins, Bombay, 1955

— Three Punch-Marked Coins from Hyderabad. JNSI. Vol.XVI, p.51, 1954.

Gupta, P.L. and Hardaker, T. Ancient Indian Silver Punch Marked Coins of the Maghada-Maurya Karsapana Series, Anjaneri, 1985.

Hardaker, T. Punchmarked Forgeries, 1988.

Kosambi, D.D. Chronological Order of Punch Marked Coins. JBBRAS. p.24, 1948-49.

Lahiri, A.N.	Numismatography of Punch-Marked Coins. JNSI.Vol.XLIX. p.155-162, 1987.
Maity, S.K.	Early Indian Coins and Currency System, Delhi,1970
Mangalam, S.J.	Local Silver Punch-Marked Coins from Maharashtra, JNSI, Vol.LV., p.12-18,
Narain, AK,	Notes on the Chronology of Punch Marked Coins. JNSI. Vol.XIX, p.19
Rajgor, D.	Minting Techniques of Punch Marked Coins of India. JNSI. Vol.LVIII, p.115-121
Ray, S.C.	A Note on the Chronology of Punch Marked Coin Hoards, JNSI, Vol.XXI, p.120
Spooner, D.B.	A New Find of Punch Marked Coins. ASR. p.150, 1905-6

CHAPTER-2

Tribal Coins of Ancient India

Introduction

Vincent A. Smith, who was a great scholar, first used the term 'Tribal Coins' in 1906 in order to issue the coins of these major communities such as the Arjunayanas, Audumbaras, Kunindas, Malvas, Nagas, Rajanyas, Yaudheyas etc. Later on Many other eminent scholars, historians and numismatist have also used the same term which Smith has used for the communities' coins.

Among these communities, the Malavas, Vrisnis and Yaudheyas used the word 'Gana' (literary means numbers or rule by many) on their coins whereas the Agreyas, Rajanyas Savitriputras, Sibis, Trigartas etc. employ the term 'Janapada'.

According to anthropological concept, a tribe is a social group usually with a definite area, dialect, culture, religion and unifying social organization. Literary sources also provide us many evidences about these 'Gana' or tribes who ruled in the north-west part of India during Alexander invasion and they fought bravely against foreigner.

Tribal Coins

Coins bearing a legend, mostly denoting the names of the issuing authority, are termed inscribed coins. These may be identified as local, tribal and monarchical issues. The local coins bear the place name and were perhaps issued by some city-state. Some coins bear the devices and the name of the king on one side and the name of the city on the other. Some of the city states known for their coins are- Varanasi, Sravasti, Kausambi, Viddehika, Ujjaini, Erakanya, Vidisa, Mahishmati, Kurara, Tripuri and the like.

The tribal republics or Janapadas like Audumbara, Kuninda and Yaudheya issued their coins in the name of their presiding deities – Mahadeva, Chitresvara and Brahmanya. The early tribal republics of the 2nd century BC refer to their names and places in Brahmi script. Some republics issued coins with their names and titles Raja or Maharaja. Copper was used as the prime metal for such issues. A few tribes issued coins in silver too. Copper coins issued in the Gandhara region bear the Brahmi inscription Negame or the Kharoshthi inscription Pancha-negame on them.

Monarchies like Surasena, Panchala, Vats and Kosal that sprang up during this period were located in the Ganga-Yamuna plain. The kingdom of Panchala issued copper coins bearing the names of no less than 35 kings. These coins have three small symbols in a row and the name of the issuer below on the obverse. On the reverse appears a figure of the deity whose name is similar to that of the ruler such as Sun for Bhanu Mitra, Indra for Indra Mitra and so on. The coins of Vatsa bear a bull with a symbol on one side, and a tree in railing together with some other symbols and the name of the king on the other. The monarchy of Kosala initially issued cast coins having a bull or an elephant before a standard on the obverse and five or six symbols on the reverse.

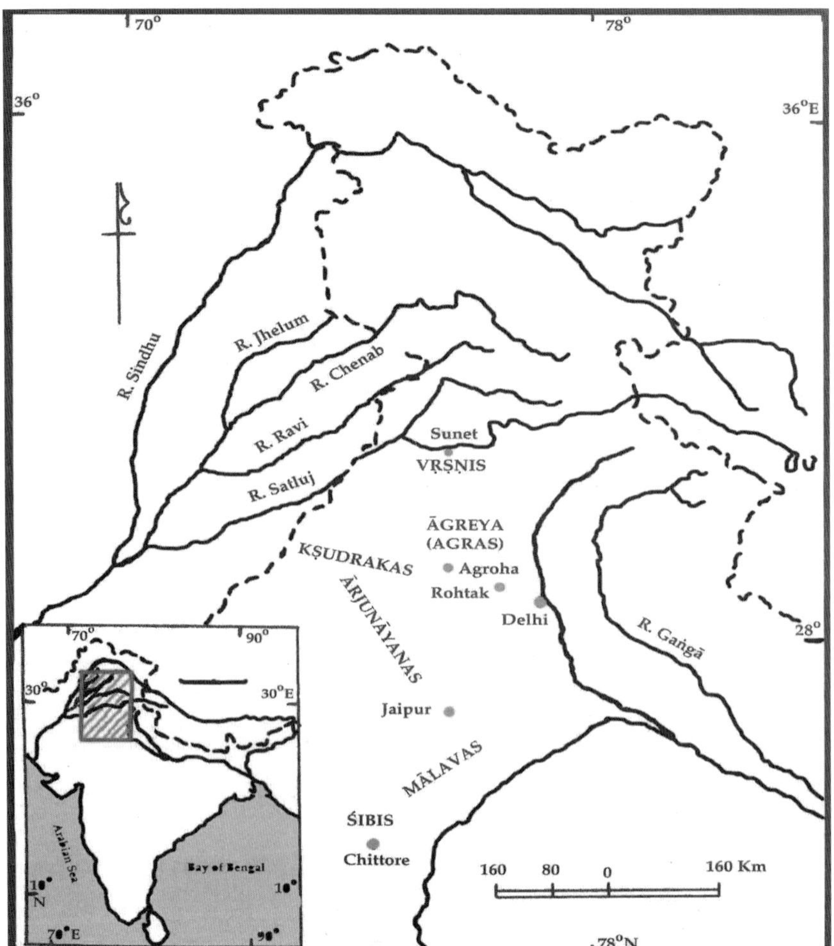

Map 2: Map showing the location of various tribes

Coins of the Arjunayanas

A great Indian grammarian, Panini called them 'Ayudhjivi in his famous book '*Astadhayayi*'. The first epigraphical evidence on Arjunayan is Prayag Prashasti of Samudragupta. It was also mentioned along with Youdheya Malava Prarjun etc. J.F. Flect connects Arjunayan with Pandav, a tribe of Punjab, mentioned by Ptolemy. Some scholars connect them with third Pandava Arjun of Mahabharat.

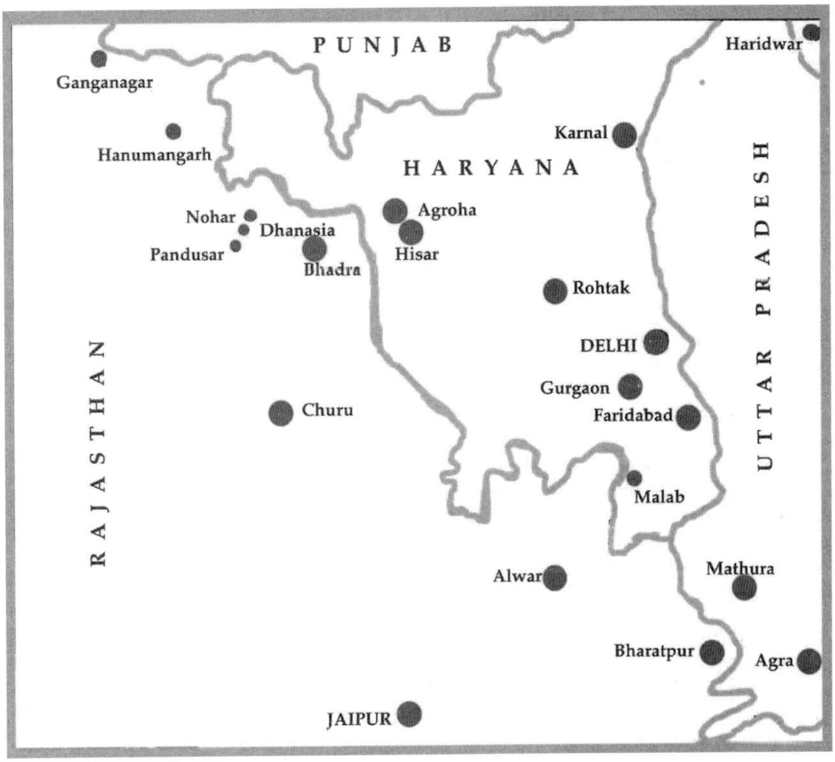

Map 3: Map showing the find spots of Agra and Arjunayana coins

Coins of Arjunayana are very rare. First piece of Arjunayana coin was published by Princep in 1834 from the collection of A. Burner. After Princep Cunningham found some copper coins of Arjunayan. Now these coins are placed in British Museum. On the basis of Prayag Prasasti, Cunningham put Arjunayan in Rajputana to the south of Madra and north of Malava. Arjunayan located in Bharatpur and Alwar district of Rajasthan by Smith. D. Handa found two copper coins of Ajunayana from the Dhanasia and Nohar in Ganganagar District of Rajasthan in 1976. These coins are examined by many scholar like Ajay Mitra Shastri, Chandra Shekhar Gupta and Ashvini Agrawal and agree with Handa attribution some coins are found of silver metal also. Nisar Ahamad the first scholar who classified Arjunayan coins in three types on the basis of legend. Now the new finding of Arjunayan coins from Nohar and Dhanasia present some new varieties. According to Handa the coins of Arjunayan are divided in four types and type four is also classified in four varieties a, b, c and d. The classification is as:

Type I

Metal: Copper

Size: Round 1.625 cm.

Weight: 81 grains-61.3 grains

Obverse: A female figure standing on dotted line between □ and tree in ⊞ railing Brahmi legend start from 10 to 2 O'clock. *Arjunayanan [am].*

Reverse: A bull on hill and turn to left.

Type II

Metal: Copper

Size: Round, 1.5 cm. to 3.625 cm.

Weight: 14.8 grain to 53 grain

Obverse: A bull standing to right before sulgava Brahmi legend *A (r) junayan [am] Jaydh.*

Reverse: An elephant to right before a tree in railing.

Type III

This type of coins is found from Nohar and Dhanasia.

Metal: Copper

Size: Oval 1.5x1.3 and one in Round, 1.4 cm.

Weight: 51 grain to 75 grain.

Obverse: Tree in railing and brahmi legend started from 7 o' clock *Arjunayan [am]*

Reverse: A figure of sitting lion to right

Type IV

Variety a:

Metal: Copper

Size: Round, 1.9 cm., 3.16 grain

Obverse: A right standing bull before sulgava. According to P.L. Gupta the legend is *Arjunayanan [am] jaya [h] D [h] amarudasa* and Nisar Ahamed read last legend as *Bhadraramas*.

Reverse: A walking elephant to right with upraised his trunk and a tree in railing a symbol of Nandipad is also seen on the top of coins.

Variety b.

Metal : Copper

Size : Round 1.95 cm.

Weight : 3.16 grain

Obverse : Same as above.

Reverse : Elephant facing tree in railing to left with upraised trunk.

Variety c.

Metal : Copper

Size : Round

Obverse : Sulagava with top curved outward

Reverse : Tree in railing with some other motifs.

Variety d.

Metal : Base Silver

Size : Round, 1.95 cm.

Weight : 45.2 grain

Obverse : Same as above.

Reverse : Walking elephant to right with raised trunk and also a tree in railing & right brick.

Coins of the Audumbaras

This tribe ruled during the first century B.C.E. This is known as udumbara or ODUMBARAS, oldest among other tribes of ancient India. The name of ODUMBARA or Audumbara is associated with the udumbara tree (Ficus glomerata).

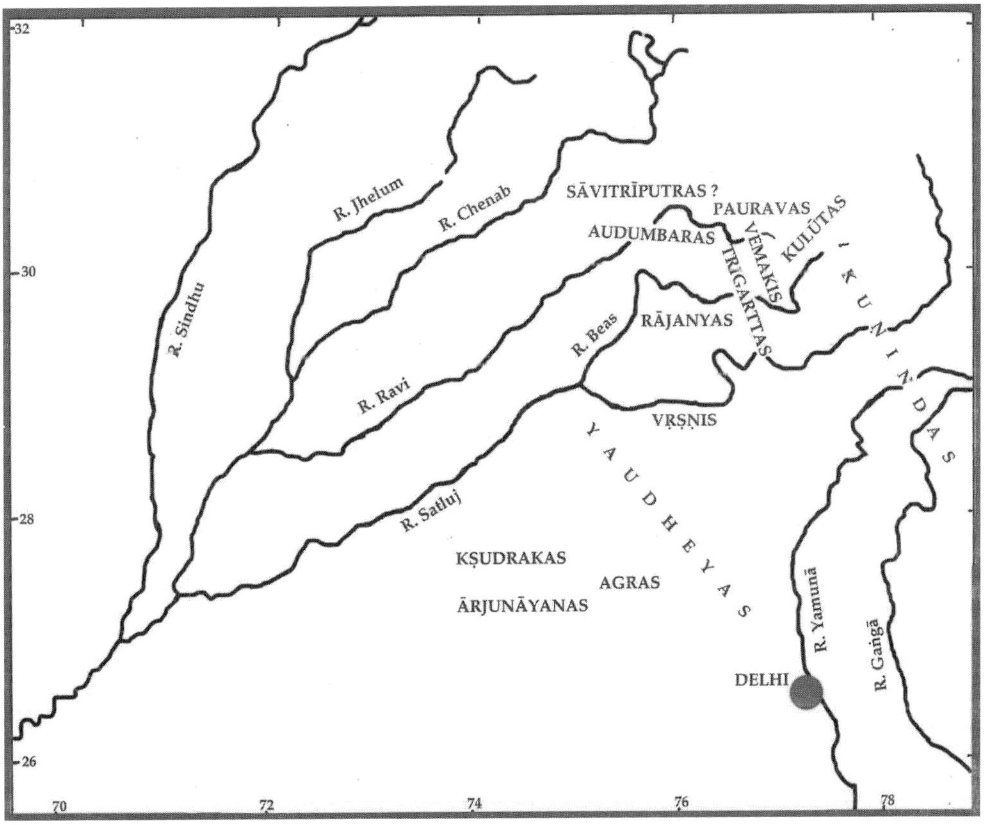

Map 4: Map showing the location of the Audumbara and other tribes

According to Panini any country where Udumbara trees found in large amount may be called Audumbara. As a result, the name Audumbara or odumbara is derived from that tree. The best example is Nurpur district which is situated between Pathankot and Kangra. We get various literary evidences of this tribe in which the earliest reference to be found in Panini's Ganpatha (c. fifth century). They have also mention in Patanjali's *Mahabhashya* a long with the Vaiyamakas, Bahlikas etc. References about Audumbaras are found in various puranas like *Vayu* (91.98) *Brahmanda* (111.66,70), *Markandeya* (58.10) etc.

The six coins of Audumbaras were discovered and published by Alexander Cunniagham. The coins that are found consists of one silver piece of Dharaghosha and five square pieces of copper during 1872-73 at Pathankot in district Gurdaspur in Punjab along with those of Zoilus, Gondophares, Kanishka and Huvishka.

The attributal coins of Sivadasa, Rudradasa and Dharaghosha were 103 in numbers. Alexander Cunningham, Chakrabarty, Allan and other scholar found attributal coins of various series. They are very few in numbers and on the basis of their metal and shape, they have been classified into two classes:-

Class I consists of the silver coins of Dharaghosh which are in round shape.

Class II consists of the copper coins of Rudradasa, Sivadasa and Dharaghosh kings which are square shaped.

The coins bear identical biscriptual legend in Brahmi and Kharoshthi.

Coins: - Legend is found in very fragmentary condition on Audumbara coins. The manufacturing) technique of Audumbara coins is Die striking. The incuse is seen well on some coins. According to Handa the coins of Audumbara are classified as.

Class I and Type I

Metal : Copper square, Wight : 1.425-1.62 gram, Size: 1.5 cm.

Obverse : Two or three storey temple with pillars, on left side a swastik symbol on railed on pillar, chakra with pendent garlands on right side.

Reverse : Elephant to left, a tree in railing, below the war line a in complete legend is found in Kharosthi *Odu[mjbara]*.

Type II and variety a and b. Type b consists the coin of odumbara king Sivadasa.

There are also two varieties of Sivadasa's coins.

Variety a: Weight 2.099 gram, size 1.474 cm.

Obverse : A trident axe on right side with storeyed temple. A legend is found in Brahmi [*Mahadevasa raja above Sivadasa* on right and *Odumbarisa* on left]

Reverse : On left a tree is in square incuse, on right a Elephant to left and a legend is found in Kharosthi [*Mahadevas raja* above] *Shivadasasa* on left [*odubarisa* on right]

Variety b : Size : 1.5x1.7cm. and weight 2.832grm.

Obverse : as above, in brahmi legend [*Mahadevasa*] *raja Siv* [*dasasa*] on right side [*odumbaris*]

Reverse : Same but a lion figure to right with upraised his tail, Three arched hill and in Kharosthi legend *Shivadasasa* is found.

Type III, Rudradasa : Rudradasa is another Audumbar king which coin is found. According to Handa his coins consists two variety: All coins of Rudradasa is put in Type-3.

Variety a:

Obverse: Same as variety a above

Reverse : Same as variety a above but the name of issuer king is found clearly on coins *Rudradasa*. Coins of Rudradasa is found in both Brahmi and Kharosthi legend. Generally the weight of all the coins of Rudradasa's of variety A is found between 2.008 gram to 3.99 gram and size in 1.57x1.51 cm to 1.25 x 1.69 cm.

Variety b.

Obverse : Same as variety A. *Odubarisa* legend is found brahmi on left and Rudradasas on right.

Reverse : As variety B of Sivadasa and in Kharosthi legend *Rudradasasa* is found to left.

Weight is found between 2.282 to 2.733 gram and size in 1.5cm to 1.57 cm. The figure of loin is also seen on reverse side of Rudradasa coins. An elephant over a wavy line is also characteristic figure of Rudradasa's coins.

Dharaghosa : Dharaghosa is anotherAudumber king which coins are found. According to Handa coins of Dharghosa in two type - 4 and type - 5.

Type - IV: Weight 2.812 grm. Size 1.692 cm.

Obverse : Same

Reverse : Same and the legend *Dharghosha* is found in Kharosthi.

Class - II

Metal : Silver, Size: 1.55cm. Round, Weight : 2.05 grm.

Obverse : Kettle drum with filleted trident left and in right side is battle axe and a figure of tree. Legend is found in brahmi (*Mahadevas rano Dharghosa* and *Odumbarisa*).

Reverse : Standing and facing with right Visvamitra holding lion skin. His right hand is raised. In Kharosti legend vispa on his left and Mitra on his right and *Mahadevasa rano Dharaghoshosa* is found.

Coins of the Kunindas

The Kunindasa occupy a very unique position in the history of ancient Indian republican tribes. The coins of this tribe are found chiefly in silver on which their name engraved stamped as Kuninda but through literary texts we get various variants of this tribe such as Kulinda, Kalinda, Kalinga, Pulinda, Kaulinda, Kauninda etc. There are numerous references of this tribe to be found in the great epics Mahabharat & Ramayan; Buddhist text

Mahamayuri; Varahmihira's Brihat Samhita; in various Puranas like the *Bhagvata*, *Brahmanda*, *Vayu* etc.

Alexander Cunnigham, a great archaeologist related the Kunindas with the moderns kunets a population of not less than 4,00,000 persons lived in the hill states which came between the Beas and Tons rivers and concluded that the Kunindas "seem to occupied the hill districts on both sides of satlej from time immemorial".

The coins of this tribe were found at Behat near Saharanpur in Uttar Pradesh in 1837 these were the earliest coins published by Prinsep in 1838. On these coins the legend that was inscribed was in Kharoshthi and Brahmi script edited by Thomas after reading Prinsep's Essays in 1858.

He translated that legend as 'of the great king Kunanda, the brothers of Amogha. Vincent Smith, a great scholar also listed total 37 coins including silver and copper of the Kunindas tribes in his Catalogue which are placed in the Indian Museum, Calcutta.

We can also found the Kuninda coins in the British Museum, London by Allan who divided the silver coins into four varieties (a-d). He ascribed these coins to first symbols that have found on the coins are; *Svastika*, a deer in the right direction with some symbols like a square with a parosal, a female figure *Lakshmi* in a standing position holding a flower in her right hand on the obverse a legend in Brahmi with a group of symbols and Kharoshthi legend on the reverse of the coins.

According to Allan, the Kuninda coins fall into two main groups. First group issued in end of the first century B.C. and other in second century A.D. Coins of group A are found in silver and copper. Legend is found in both Brahmi on obverse side and in kharosthi on reverse side.

Coins of Amoghabhuti: Coins of Amoghabhuti are found both in silver and copper. Silver coins of Amoghabhuti consists four variety. All coins are in round shape. The character figure of Amoghabhuti coins may be described as follow:

Variety a :

Obverse : A standing female figure (Laxmi), (some times on lotus. She hold a lotus in her right hand. Deer to right. Three arched hill is above the back of clear. In brahmi legend '*Rajnath Kunindsya Amoghabhutisy a Mohara Jasya*'.

Reverse : Swastik symbol, Nandipade, indrayasti. Six arched hill and a tree in railing are seen on reverse and legend is found in Kharosthi '*Rana Kunimdasa Amoghabhutis Maharajas*'.

The weight of variety a are found between 29 grain to 34 grain and size in .65 to 7 inch.

Variety b :

Weight 34.4 grain size .7 inch

Obverse : as same, Swastik symbol below deer three arched hill and legend found in brahmi.

Reverse : Same as above. Legend in Kharosthi.

Variety c: is also same but there is no any symbol below the deer. In Brahmi '*Ku*' legend is found below a animal on variety d. Three arched hill is also found below deer.

According to Allan, copper coins of Amoghabhuti consists two class. Those coins which are made of neat fabric and found with good and complete legend are included in class I. Class II consists coins with some wornness. Legend which is inscribed on these coins is incomplete.

Symbol like *Swastika*, *Nandipada* or water pot are found on some new varieties of Kuninda coins. These symbols are seen between deer and goddess. Coins of Kuninda are found in both manufacturing technique, Die struck and Cast.

Coins of the Yandheyas

In ancient Indian tribes, Yaudheya is a very prominent figure. The word 'yaudheya' is looking derived from *yudha* (strike) are famous as a brave warriors in ancient Indian History. According to V.S. Agrawala, the first refer Astadhyayi gives us first reference about this tribe. In Astadhyayi yaudheya are mentioned as an 'ayudhjivi sangha' cunnigham connected yaudheya to yudhisthir, king of Pandav, on the evidence of Mahabharat. After the date of Pushyamitra Shung, Yaudheya decleared their independence. They faced some trouble when Indo-Greek attacked under Menandar. They regained power and fond new capital Naurangabad. They also setup a mint in their capital. Several inscriptions of yaudheyas come out in light. Rohatak, Vijaygarh, Agroha are famous for finding their inscriptions.

Coins:

In 1936, Allan was the first scholar who classified yaudheyas coins in six classes. According to Allan, Class I consists five varieties. Handa is not, agree with Allan's classification. According to Handa, class I consist four varieties.

Class - A

Variety a :

Copper : Square, 1.27 cm. weight 615 gram

Obverse : Bull to right and legend [*Yo*] *dh* [*e*] *Y* [*a*] [*am*] is found in Brahmi

b :

Copper : rectangular, 7.5 x 15 m.m., weight 2 gram

Obverse : A legend *yodheyanam* is sound in early brahmi characters is found over a humped bull to right.

Reverse : Obliterated

c:

Copper : Size round size 1.25 to 1.75 cm. and weight 9.5 gram to 15.7 grain.

Obverse : legend in brahmi '*yadheyanam* and a humped bull walking to right

Reverse : Obliterated

d :

Copper : circular, 1.5 cm., weight 0.8 gram

Obverse : motif of bull before post of centre, legend in brahmi *yodheyanam.*

Reverse : A figure of elephant walking to left with upraised trunk.

Class- 2

According to Handa, class II of yodheya coins is more rich than other classes. There are sixteen varieties of coins in class- II from A to P. Approximately all coins are made of copper and potin.

All the coins of this variety are found in round shape size between 1.25 cm. to 2.25 cm. and weight between 1.16 gram to 4.482 gram. Bull animal is found on obverse side of yodheya coins either to left or to right before a *yupa*. Legend in brahmi '*Bahudhanyake yodheyanam*' is found on obverse of coins. On reverse side figure of an elephant is seen to right or to left with trunk. The characteristic figures of class- III is motif six headed Kartikeya is found on Yodheya's silver and copper coins. A gold coins of this class is also come out in light by Handa. In brahmi legend, *Bhagavata-suamino Brahmanya*' found in fragmentary condition of this class. Some variety show the figure of Shiva replacing Kartikeya. Class 4 is a lies with legend (*Bhanuvarmasa*). Class V is a single square copper coins. On obverse side coins represents a bull and a legend is found in brahmi character '*youdheyanam*'. Class VI represents Kartikeya figure. which made in copper and also a legend '*youdheyanam-ganasya-jaya*' is found in Kushana brahmi characters. Handa conscribed some new varieties of youdheya coins. On reverse side of class VI, is found *Devsena*.

Local coins:

Vincent Smith was the first scholar who used the term, 'Local coins' for those coins which were introduced by Nigam or monorchial states like Vidisa, Eran, Kausambi, Ayodhya, Mathura and Panchala. Numismatist put them from second century B.C. to fourth century A.D. These coins are made up of copper and in round or square. According to Bela Lahiri all the coins of local series are issued by indigenous authority or monarchial states parallel like youdheya, Audembara, Arjunayana tribe.

Kausambi :

In sixth century B.C. Kausambi was the capital of Vats., among one of the sixteen Mahajanpadas. According to Puranas, Nichakshu the grandson of Janmejay founded this city after washing away by river Ganga to Hastinapura. The great audha Bihara Jetwana was also here which was bought by a merchant and gave it to Baudha Bhikkhu in Dan. Not only religious point of view but also the importance of this city for mart and Trade. Merchants came here from Magadha, Kosala and from south part of India.

On the basis of epic and Puranas, Cunnigham identified Kausambi with modern Kosam village, 130 miles south-east from Allahabad. This identification has been also proved from finding city type coins, with Kosambi legend. There are so many varieties seen in Kausambi coins. All the Local coins of Kausambi are made of copper and bronze. Allen devided Kausambi coins in two group on the basis of manufacturing technique. First group is made in cast technique and other in die struck.

The basic prominent figure of Kausambi coins are Bull and Tree in railing. According to Bela Lahiri coins of Kausambi consist four class. Class I is of early round cast pieces. The majority of this class one of inscribed coins. They used as city type coins. Some are also found from here bearing the name 'Kausambi'. Weight of this class we find between 29 grain to 152.5 grain and size 1 inch to 1.1 inch. Indrayasti bull or elephant is found on obverse side and six arch hill, *Nandipad*, *Ujjaini* symbol and *swastik* are found on reverse. According to Allan all these coins belong to third century B.C. class II represents the manufacturing technique of coins in Die-struck. Class II, IIIrd are a long series of inscribed coins; which are introduce by Dev, Mitra and Magha rullars. Dev and Mitra rulers rulled over Kausambi from second century B.C. till flourishing Kushana empire. Weight of Mitra and Deva kings coins of Kausambi are found between 7 grain to 190 grain and size in 4 inch to 1 inch.

Coins series of class IV is belong to Magha dynasty, who defeated Kushana and held their power on Kausambi. They rulled over Kausambi circa 129 A.D. to 250 A.D. Both coins and inscriptions are found from Kausambi and Rewa region. Bhimsena, Bhadramagha Shivamagha, Bhimavarman etc. like Magha king came in lite by finding their coins.

All the coins of Magha Rullars are made of copper. Coins of Magha kings are in round or irregular square shape. Size of round coins 1 cm. to 1.5 cm. and irregular square are found between 1.2 x 1.4 cm. to 2.8 x 2 cm. and weight found between 1.7 gram to 3.8 gram. On reverse side of coins hill, tree and name of kings in brahami legend are found. Reverse side of magha coins, represents a lanky bull, to right or left.

Mathura:

In Mahajanpad era, Mathura was the capital of Surasena now situated on the right bank of Jamuna in District Mathura in Uttar Pradesh. It is 270 miles long away from Kausambi in north west. Mahabharata and Puranas narrates that Mathura belonged to yadav clan. Great Greek writer Megasthenes wrote about Mathura which give us important information that Mathura was rulling under Mauryan administration.

According to *Yugapurana*, after the decline of Mauryan empire, Mathura came under Yavanas for short time. Pushyamitra founder of shunga empire freed Mathura from Yavanas. After the study of coins we can devided Mathura coins in two group. Group I represents the local kings of Mathura like mitra ending name.

Among thirteen local rullars, twelve local kings belong to mitra and datta ending name and last thirteenth local kings name of mathura is Balbhuti. Second group represent Saka- Kshatrapa king of Mathura.

Dipiction of Gaja-Laxmi is found on coins of Gomitra and Suryamitra. Ujjaini and srivats are very symbol. Weight of mitra prominent coins are between 22 grain to 145 grain and size between 5 inch to 85 inch Gomitra I, Gomitra II, Suryamitra, Brahmmitra Dridhamitra, Vishnumitra and Satyamitra are came in this category. Weight of Datta, rullars coins (Purushadatta, Ramdatta, Uttamdatta, Kamadatta, Bhavadatta, etc. are found between 42 grain to 137.3 grain and size between .35 inch to .8 inch. Last local rullars of Mathura Balbhuti's coin is found between 33 grain to 66.5 grain. Name of Mathura kings in brahmi legend are found on obverse with Gaja-Laxmi, tree and fish with river. On the reverse of Mathura local coins, figure of tree, elephants with rider are found.

Coins of Ayodhya and Panchala:

The city of Ayodhya is now lies in Faizabad District in Uttar Pradesh. In Epic era it was the capital of kingdom Kosala. At that time this city was situated on the bank of river Sarayu moern Ghagara Another two great city Saketa and Sravasti were included in Kosala kingdom. In sixth century B.C. both Saketa and Sravasti were included amongst six great cities of India. Now Saketa, identified with modern Sujankot and Sravasti with Sahet-Mahet. The Local dynastic Coins of Ayodhya fall in two class. These are inscribed with rulers name. One is square cast and another is round struck. All the coins of class first are similar in style and type. Bull or rarely an elephant is found on obverse side of class first and reverse consists five or six symbol like, 'Ujjaini' symbol, tree in railing four Handipad, swastik etc. Generally the issuar name is found in prakrit like Muldeva Nayudeva, Visakhadeva, Dhanadeva, Sivadatta and Hardatta another depiction abhiseka of Laksmi is found on Visakhadeva and Sivadatta.

Second class of coins belong to die struck and were issued by other family who rulled over this reign after Kusana being Kaniska I or in half of the second century A.D. They are Ajvarman, Ayumitra, Devamitra, Kumudsena, Madhavavapman, Sanghamitra, Satgmitra and Vijaymitra. On obverse side of coins bear a figure. of Bull and a cock or nandipada on reverse. The last local dynastic coins of Ayodhya are found till the rise of Gupta in beginning of the fourth century A.D. The weight of local Ayodhya coins generally found between 9.5 grain to 136.5 and size between .4 inch to .9 (round diestrck), (.4 x .4 inch to .9 x .8 inch) square coins.

Panchala was associated with Kuru at the time of Mahabharat. Three district of U.P., Barailly, Badaun and Farrukhabad come under the region of ancient Panchala. *Divyavadan*, *Jataka* and also *Mahabharat* give geographical dividation of Panchal in two part, North and South Panchal.Ahichchatra and Kampilya were capital of boths two kingdom. Ancient Ahichchatra is associated with modern Ramanagar village. Panchal was one of the sixteen Mahajanpada during Buddha time. According Allan, The coins attributed to Punchala, 'forms one of the longest and most uniform series of ancient India. The reverse side of Panchala coins are very useful for the iconographical study on the obverse side, In square incuse, three most prominent symbol of Panchal coins are depicted and Belong this symbol, the issuers name are found in shungs style brahmi character. Most of Penchala rulers are Mitra-ending name as Agnimitra, Anamitra, Phalgunimitra, Sarymitra, Indramitra, Bhanumitra, Bhumimitra, Brahmamitra, Baha satimitra, Jaygupta, Bamgata, Rudraghosa, Vagapala, Vasusen etc. We can arranged in six group according their ending name I. Mitra ending name, II Ghosa ending name III Gupta ending name, IV Sen ending name, V. Nandi ending and VI Pal ending name. The reverse side of Panchala coins are very interesting. There is found a great similarity between issuer's name and depicted god on reverse of Panchala coins. Generly the weight of Panchala coins found in range between 12.5 to 273 grain and size between .45 to 1.05 in inch.

References

Bajpai, K.D.	Indian Numismatics Studies, New Delhi, 2004
Dasgupta, K.K.	A Tribal History of Ancient India: A Numismatics Approach, Kolkata,1974
—	A Unique Silver Coins of the Arjunayanas, JNSI. Vol.XXXIX, p.49-51
Gupta, L.C.	Some Rare Kuninda Coins, JNSI. Vol.XLVII, p.36-40
Gupta, P.	Geography from Ancient Indian Coins & Seals, New Delhi, 1989
Handa,D.	Tribal Coins of Ancient India, New Delhi, 2006
—	A New Type of Arjunayana Coins, JNSI. Vol.XLI, p.23-27
Maity, S.K.	*Early Indian Coins and Currency System, Delhi, 1970*
Mukherjee, D.	A Note on the Some New Coins of the Audumbaras and the Yaudheyas, JNSI. Vol.XLV, p. 20-22
Narain, A.K.	Seminar Paper on the Local Coins of Northern India c. 300 B.C to 300 A.D, Varanasi, 1968
Prakash, P.	Significance of Animal Motif on Kuninda Coins, JNSI. Vol.XXXVIII, Pt.-I, p.110-112
Sharan, M.K.	Tribal Coins: A Study, Delhi, 1972
Singh, J.P and Ahmad Nisar	Seminar Paper on the Tribal Coins of Ancient India c.200 B.C to 400 A.D, Varanasi, 1977
Singh, O.P.	Temple Architecture on Audumbra Coins, JNSI. Vol.XXXIV, pt-II, p.196-200
Sircar, D.C.	Studies in Indian Coins, New Delhi, 2008
Smith, V.A.	Catalogue of the Coins in the Indian Museum, Calcutta, 1906

CHAPTER-3

Indo-Greek Coins

Greeks initiated a new phase in the history of Indian numismatics and a major part of their history is reconstructed on the evidence of the coins. Alexander entered Babylon, the capital of Persian Empire, shortly after the battle of Gaugameles in 331 BC. The mint of Babylon which had earlier struck Persian Darics and Sigloi, started stricking coins for Alexander and remained his chief eastern mint. He followed Darius across Iran during 330 BC, then spent most of the time subduing the north eastern satrapies of Bactra and Sogdiana. The Achaemenids had not minted coins in these regions but Alexander had opened a mint at Bactra (Balkh: Zarispar) where he spent the winter of 329-328 BC. In 327 he marched south through the Kabul Valley, where he had already found a new city during the winter of 330-329 BC. and continued to northern Pakistan and Punjab where he was campaining until he commenced his return journey in 325 BC. Alexander reached Babylon in 324 and died there in June 323 BC. He did not leave behind any permanent settlements in India. But a second Greek Invasion from Bactria , more than a century after his death, led to the establishment of Greek rule in north western India. Alexander began issuing tetradrachms with a head of Hercules wearing a lion skin headdress on the obverse and seated Zeus on the reverse some years before his arrival in Babylon during 331 BC. These coins together with other companion silver denominations and associated gold and copper series, were issued at many mints from Babylon westwards and are therefore described as his general coinage. In contrast with Alexander's general coinage these lion issues were apparently struck to satisfy local currency requirements in Babylonia.

Euthydemos, c 230 to 190 B.C.

Euthydemos obtained the kingdom of Bactro-Sogdiana by force and was latter combating Antiochos III during the years 208 to 206 BC. There are number of numismatic evidence show that Euthydemos conquered the kingdom from Diodotos II and that he was succeeded by Demetrios whose reign ended c. 171 BC. Another numismatic evidence show that

Euthydemos reorganized the coinage and the distinctive feature of this re-organisation was a change in the orientation of the die axes on the coins.

Demetrius, c.205 to 190 to 171 B.C.

Demetrius was the son of Euthydemos and in 190 BC he succeeded his father as king.However he was already a king during his father's lifetime. Demetrius issued two different series of coins in Bactria , a common series with a "standing Hercules" reverse type struck at most mints and a much rare series with 'standing Athena' on the reverse that was only struck in chief workshops of the Balkh mints.

Map 5: Map showing Indo Greek Kingdom in North West South Asia

Demetrius began his reign as king of Bactria and Margiana but he ended his reign as king of a much larger empire.He also struck new bilingual currency in both silver and copper on a new Indo-Greek weight standard.These were (Greek/Karoshti) silver drachms weighing 2.42 grams.Demetrius and subsequent Indo-Greek kings issued separate series of coins for their Bactrian province and for their territories lying south of Hindu Kush.

Such coins could not easily be integrated with pre existing currency of conquered Indian territories either economically or culturally.They were illegible to the Indigenous Indian population who wrote in Brahmi and Karosthi.

Euthydemos II,c.190 to 171 B.C.

Euthydemos II was son of Demetrius and only struck coins in Bactria where he used the same mints as his father:- *Merv , Balkh and Panjhir*. He is depicted as young man on his coins that have parallel die axes.These two features along with his use of a standing Hercules reverse type serve to differentiate his coins from those struck by his grandfather Euthydemos I.

Eucratides c. 171 B.C.

Soon after Eucratides had revolted (c.171 B.C.) he eliminated Demetrius and his son Euthydemos II but he did not succeed in putting an end to the dynasty founded by Euthydemos. Antimachos who was contemporary of Demetrius succeeded the throne along with two young associate kings Agathocles and Pantaleon.

For a period this legitimate trio controlled the main mints in Bactria where they struck a series of pedigree coins. Coins of Ecraticles struck during the early period of this reign bear the standing figure of Apollo on their reverse and the simple inscription of king Eucratides but at a slightly later date he adopted an honorific title :- "*great king Eucratides*" "The Saviour King Eucratides" which was placed on his coins.

Agathocles began issuing bilingual Greek Brahmi coins at Pushakalavati shortly before his final expulsion from Bactria by Eucratides.Eucratides was ruling a united and prosperous Indo-Greek kingdom that lasted until the nomad migration of c.130 B.C.which removed most of the north Afghan plateau from the Indo-Greek territory.Instead of restricting the associate kingship to his sons he started elevating successful military commanders to the rank of king.From 160 to c.130 B.C. only two kings **eucratides and heliocles** wielded authority over the whole Indo-Greek realm.

Heliocles c. 160 to c. 130 B.C.

Heliocles, the immediate successor of Eucratides was ruling when the Scythians occupied much of northern Afghanistan about 130 B.C. Heliocles was the last king who struck Attic tetradrachms in a Bactrian mint. It was a common Greek practice for a grandson to be named after his grandfather. Kings like Apollodotus and Menander who were associated to Eucratides and Heliocles wielded great power and were of far greater local importance then the supreme kings who probably had his seat in Bactria.

Eucratides stuck such a large number of bilingual copper coins that they rank among the commonest Indo-Greek copper issues of the 2nd century B.C.

Apollodotus and Menanader

When Eucratides conquered northern Pakistan he appointed two kings, Apollodotus was the only Indo-Greek king after Agathacles and Pantaleon who struck coins of distinctively Indian type. The rectangular bilingual drachms bear an eastern control marks and show in addition to Greek King that the standard Greek and Karosthi legends of Apollodotus and his Elephant /Bull designs, a group of symbols commonly used on local Indian coins but unknown elsewhere on Indo-Greek coins.

The Indian symbols used by Apollodotus are, a three arched Buddhist stupa, a river symbol, the sun, a form of 6 arm symbols and a Taurine symbol.

Early Brahmi Inscription of Menanader at Reh

D.P. Sharma has brought to light a Brahmi inscription from Reh. This inscription is inscribed on the lower part of a broken pillar, which is converted into a Shiva Linga. The villagers have erected a rectangular argha around the Linga recently. Broken pillar is made of dark coloured (Chunar) sandstone where as the argha is in light red colour. There are only four lines in the said inscription. The three lines are complete and the fourth is party blurred. The language of the inscription is Prakrit and its script is Brabmi of Sunga. In the first three lines titles of a king are mentioned. On the basis of the these titles it ìanbe surmised that this inscription belonged to a foreign Indo-Greek, Saka-parthian or Kusana King who was ruling between late second century BC in the Ganga-Yamuna doab. The inscription reads as follows:

1. MAHARAHSA RAJRAJASA
2. MAHANSA TRATARASDHAMI
3. KASJAYA TAS CHA A PRA
4. JIJASA............................ RAS.......................................

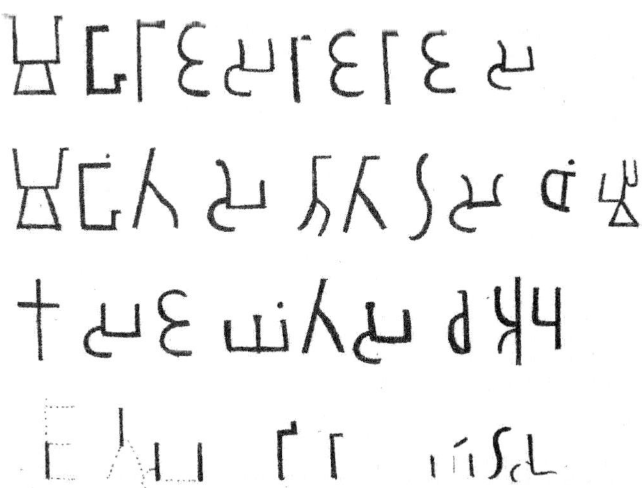

Reh inscription of Indo-Greek king Menander mid second c.BC

On the basis of paleography this inscription can has been dated between 150 B.C. and 100 B .C. Professor G.R. Sharma read the name of Menander in fourth line and he concluded that this inscription belongs to bzdo-Greek King Menander I. Some leading historians and paleographic experts are of the opinion that the Reh inscription does not belong to the Indo Greek King Meandar I but to some *Saka Palhav*, Kusana who was ruling in the beginning of the Christian era. If it may be assumed that the Re/i inscription belonged to the indo king Menander. However, this is posthumous inscription of Menanderlwhich was inscribed by his wife and son. The fourth line is partly broken the reading Jitasa Minderas maybe correct but this is conjectural the possibility of a war between Indo-Greek and the Sungas at *Reh* situated just at the confluence of Rind and Ywmuza, possible. In spite of hardwork of S.K. Muttu., l.A .S. now Duptty chief secretary Government of Uttranchal . The then additional district magistrate of Fatehpur ande author the Reh inscription was buried under a cemented platform in a modem temple by the local people 7 March 1979. They did it under the impression that it was the ancient Shiva Linga.

Menander and Strato

The reign of Menander was central in understanding the history of Indo-Greeks.He was definitely the most important Greek king that ever ruled Indian territories.

The immediate successor of Menander are Agathocleia and Strato I. It is generally agreed that queen Agathacleia, whose name and portrait appear on a number of coins in conjunction with those of his son Strato, was the wife of Menander.The widowed queen was regent during the infancy of her son Strato. On the first series of coins the portrait of Agathocleia together with her name in Greek appears on the obverse, while the name and the titles of Strato in Kharoshthi, without portrait, are relegated to the reverse.

Type of Coins of Indo Greek

Euthydemus

Metal - Gold

Wt. - 7.8 gm

Size - 1.9 cm

Obverse - Olademed Bust of young Euthydemos I Right.

Reverse - Hercules Naked sat on a rock Facing on the left, Holding his club. Greek Legend BASICEOS EUTHEDEMOY.

Euthydemus

Metal - Silver

Wt - 14.4 gm

Size - 2.9 cm

Obverse - Head of the king Right

Reverse - Herakles, bearded naked, seated left on sock on which is spread lion's skin, in right hand, club which rests on his knee.

Demetruus

Metal - Silver

Wt - 14.2 gm

Size - 2.9 cm

Obverse - In centre : Diademed bust of king within a border.

Reverse - IN centre – Athena standing facing with spear and shueld, Greek legand on right and left- BASILEOS DEMETRIOY.

Demetrius

Metal - Copper

Wt - 6.7 gm

Size - 2.3 cm

Obverse - In centre Bearded bust of Hercules, club Resting on Shoulder within a beaded border.

Reverse - In centre, Artemis standing with bow : drawing arrow from quiver, Greek legand on Right and left – BASILEOS DEMETRLOY.

Euthydemus II

Metal - Silver

Wt - 14.5 gm

Size - 3.4 cm

Obverse - Diademed and draped Bust of Euthydemos II right Herakles standing facing, Holding oak wreath, Club and lion's skin, Monogram to inner left.

Reverse - Greek legand on Right and left- BASILEOS EUTHEOEMOY

Eucratides I

Metal - Silver

Wt - 15.9 gm

Size - 3.2 cm

Obverse - Bust of Eucratides, Helmet decorated with Bull's Horn and ear, within bead and Red border.

Reverse - Depiction of the Dioscuri, each Holding Plam in left Hand, spear in Righthand and Greek legand BASILEOS MEGALOV EUKRATIDOV.

Eucratides

Metal - Copper

Wt - 7.1 gm

Size - 1.6 cm

Obverse - Bust of the king Right, diademed, without Helmet, Greek legand- BASILEOS EUKRATIDOV.

Reverse - Nike left, Bearing wreath and plam Kharoshthi legand – Maharajasa Evukratidasa.

Heliodes

Metal - Silver

Wt - 14.0 gm

Size - 3.2 cm

Obverse - In centre : Bust of king within a read Border.

Reverse - Zeus standing Holding Scepter and thunder bolt, Greek legand – BASILEOS DIKAIOY HLIOKLEOS.

Appolodotus I

Metal - Silver

Wt - 2.4 gm

Size - 1.6 x 2.0 cm

Obverse - In centre : Elephant, Greek legand- BASILEOS Apdlodotoy SUTHROS.

Reverse - Bull, Kharoshthi legand : Maharajasa Apaladatasa tratarasa.

Menander

Metal - Silver

Wt - 9.2 gm

Size - 2.5 cm

Obverse - Helmeted Bust of King Greek legand : BASILEOS SUTHROS MENANOROY.

Reverse - Pallas standing Holding Shield and Hurling thunderbolt, Kharoshthi legand – Maharajasa Tratarasa Menandrasa.

Menanda

Metal - Copper

Wt - 7.7 gm

Size - 2.2 x 2.7 cm

Obverse - Helmet Head of Pallas, Greek legand – BASILEOS SUTHROS MENANDROY.

Reverse - Shield with gorgon Head, Kharoshthi legand : Maharajasa tratarasa Menandrasa.

Strato

Metal - Silver

Wt - 2.4 gm

Size - 1.6 cm

Obverse - Helmeted bust of king Greek legand – BASILEOS EPIPHANOYS STRATONOS.

Reverse - Pallas standing Holding shield and Hurling thunderbolt Knaroshti legand : Maharajasa Prakachasa tratarasa stratasa.

References

Bivar, A.D.H. — Bactrian Treasure from Qunduz, JNSI. Vol.XVII, Pt-I, p.37-52

Chaudhary, K. — Dionysis of Indo-Greek Coins: A Study, JNSI. Vol.XLV, p.119-133

Cunningham, A. — Coins of Alexander Successors in the East, London, 1873

— Coins of the Indo-Sythians, London, 1892

— Coins of the Later Indo-Sythians, London, 1894

Gardner, P. — Catalogue of the Coins of the Greek and Scythic Kings of Bactria and India (in the British Museum) , London, 1886

Jash, P. — Religion as Reflected in the Indo-Greek Coinage, JNSI. Vol.L, p.58-63

Jenkins, G.K. — Some Recent Indo-Greek Accessions of the British Museum, JNSI. Vol.XXX, p.23-27

Kundu, P. — Indian Deities on Bactrian and Indo-Greek Coins, JNSI. Vol.XLIV, p.130-135

Lahiri, A.N. — Corpus of Indo-Greek Coins, Calcutta, 1965

— Religio-Mythical Bearing of the Representation of Zeus on Indo-Greek Coins, JNSI. Vol.XLII, Pt. I, p.58-65

— The So Called Joint Coins of the Indo-Greeks, JNSI. Vol.XXXIX, p.69-76

Narayan, A.K. — The Indo-Greek, Oxford, 1957

— The Coin Types of Indo-Greek Kings, JNSI. Vol.XVI, Pt-II, p.293. ff.

The Hindu Divinities on the Coinage of Agathocles, JNSI. Vol.XXXV, p.73-77

Oikonomides, AL.N. — Soter the Great: Last of the Indo-Greek Kings, JNSI. Vol.XXXV, p.82-89

Pandey, D.B. — Notes on Indo-Greek Coins, JNSI. Vol.XXVIII, Pt-II, p.198-200

Singh, J.P. — A Religious Study of the Indo-Greek Coins, JNSI. Vol.XXXIII, Pt-II, p.8-23

Tarn, W.W. — Greek in Bactria and India, Cambridge, 1951

Trivedi, H.V. — Some Interesting Indo-Bactrian Coins, JNSI. Vol.XIII, Pt-I, p.78-91

Whitehead, R.B. — Catalogue of the Coins in the Punjab Museum, Lahore , Vol.I, Indo-Greek Coins, Oxford, 1914

— *Indo-Greek Numismatics,* Argonaut, Chicago, 1970

— *www.vcoins.com*

— www.geocities.com

— www.wikipedia.org

CHAPTER-4

Roman Coins in India

27 BC, the traditional date of the beginning of the Roman Empire, saw no radical change in the coinage. Late Imperatorial issues were very much like the first coins of Caesar Augustus as emperor. The assumption of the title *Augustus* (revered one) merely confirmed the position that Octavian had held since the defeat of Antony at Actium in 31 B.C. Rulers following Augustus would also assume this title as the identifying mark of the Emperor. Our examples below will skim the surface of Roman *Imperial* coins from the beginning of the Empire until the death of Commodus in the late 2nd century A.D. Later pages will extend this date to the end of the Empire. Most of the significant terms have been covered on the earlier pages of this series. These will be reinforced and joined by a few more. So vast a subject can hardly be covered with so small a page but the beginning student will be able to derive from these samples a general overview of Roman Imperial coins.

Caesar Augustus. AR Denarius, 27-24 BC. On our first coin Octavian has assumed the title of Augustus. Whether called Octavian, Caesar or Augustus, this one man required no introduction to the Roman man on the street. Titles are minimal. The anepigraphic obverse shows a dignified portrait of a simple bare head facing right. Judging from coins of his earlier years, the portrait is a bit idealized. At the time this coin was struck Augustus was about 40. Few of his coins show age progression. The reverse shows a Capricorn, Augustus' sign of the zodiac, with rudder and globe steering the course of history. Above, a *cornucopia*, horn of plenty, promises good times to come. Behind the head is a circular punch mark testing the coin and proving it solid. Earlier coins of Augustus fit better into the style of the Imperatorial period than they do in the Imperial. His later coins adopted the *encircling legends* that were to become standard as will be seen on the remainder of the coins on this page.

Caligula, Bronze Sestertius, As and Quadrans, 39-40 AD, 37-38 AD and 40-41 AD The first four Emperors following Caesar Augustus were members of his extended family, the *Julio-Claudians*. Tiberius, Caligula, Claudius and Nero, through a tangled web of adoptions, claimed kinship with Augustus and his adopted father Julius Caesar. Many coins of the period bore extensive legends spelling out exactly who was the ruler and what gave him the right to rule. Bronze coins were issued from the largest, the *Sestertius* or 1/4 denarius, to the smallest the *Quadrans* or 1/64 denarius. Most sestertii bore the portrait of the ruler (we show an exception) while quadrantes used simpler types. Our sestertius (27.6g) shows a seated figure of Pietas, personification of piety, surrounded by the (expanded) legend running *clockwise* starting at the lower left : C(aius) CAESAR DIVI AVG(ugusti) PRON(epos) AVG(ustus) P(ontifex) M(aximus) TR(ibunicia) P(otestas) III P(ater) P(atriae) and, in exergue, PIETAS. This translates: Gaius Caesar, Great-grandson of the Divine Augustus, Chief Priest, with the Power of a Tribune, Father of his Country. Significant among the titles is the spelling out that Gaius was descended from the god-Augustus and was himself Augustus. At any one time there were many priests but only one was the highest, Maximus. TRP was an office related to the Republican Tribune of the People who had the power of veto over actions of the Senate. In the Republic, this office was held for one year so the Emperors renewed the title every year and marked the number on their coins with a numeral following TRP. The first year was TRP with no numeral; year two TRP II etc. Emperors of the first century advanced the number on the anniversary date of their assumption of the first TRP. Several different systems would be used by later rulers. This sestertius with TRP III dates from March, 39, to March, 40. Father of his Country was an honorary title traditionally accepted a while after the beginning of the reign and always last in the series of titles shown. The appearance of Pietas on the coin declares that Caligula (a nickname by which Gaius is known to history to distinguish him from many other rulers named Gaius) was doing his pious duty in a manner which would be explained on the reverse of this coin. Here we see Caligula sacrificing over an altar while two attendants stand by with a bull (to be the next sacrifice). In the background we see the newly completed Temple of the Divine Augustus.

This *Commemorative* coin was issued for several years to reinforce the position of Caligula as the natural successor of Augustus who was still remembered and revered by most Romans. The reverse legend is across field: DIVO AVG (to the Divine Augustus). Also across field is SC (Senatus Consulto - by decree of the Senate). SC was used on almost every issue of bronze coins during the Imperial period. Scholars have argued several theories about why this use was so universal and why it was on so few silver issues. We will leave it with the note that it is to be expected on bronze coins and wait for better evidence on the exact reason for SC. The example quadrans (3.1g) weighs considerably more that the 1/16 of the sestertius that one might expect. The reason for this is that it was struck in (relatively) pure (red) *copper* rather than the more valuable *orichalcum*, the (yellow) brass alloy used for the sestertius. When new the two coins would have been greatly different in color but the toning of the different metals often leaves the two hard to distinguish without cleaning the coin to a point that would ruin its value to collectors. It is customary to refer to all copper alloy coins as AE or Aes, the Latin word for bronze. They are sold as 'bronzes' without regard to exactly which alloy was used. Later in the Imperial period the distinction between the metals weakened to the point that all coins were more or less the same alloy, usually a leaded bronze. The obverse type is a cap of Liberty of a style traditionally given to freed slaves. The reverse center shows RCC (Remissa ducentesima - Remitting the 200th) referring to Caligula's repeal of a .5% sales tax. The legends *C CAESAR DIVI AVG PRON AVG SC/ COS TERT PON M TRP IIII PP* add only the title of *Consul* followed by the ordinal 3rd rather than the more usual Roman numeral III. Consulships were assumed on the first day of the year so this combined with TRP IIII assigns the coin to the period March to December, 40 AD. Emperors did not always assume the consulship (highest office of the old Republic) every year so the COS dating is not always as good a dating device as it is here for Caligula who assumed COS IIII in January, 41 AD. Quadrantes are relatively common during the first century but cease to be issued shortly after the middle of the second century. Inflation seems to have made the small denomination unnecessary. Also struck in copper, our third coin (10.3g) is a portrait As (plural asses - 1/4 sestertius or 4 quadrantes) with reverse showing Vesta, goddess of the hearth. This example has *Patinated* an attractive green color hiding the red copper color it had when new. The obverse legend *C CAESAR AVG GERMANICVS PON M TR POT* honors Caligula's father Germanicus. Struck in the first year of his reign, this coin bears no numeral following TR POT. Note also that the coin lacks the title PP which had not yet been assumed. Vesta asses are the most commonly seen portrait coin of this popular Emperor.

Ve-spasian, AR Denarius, 75 AD Following the death of Nero, last of the Julio-Claudian Emperors, civil war resulted in five emperors reigning in 68-69 AD. The eventual winner was Titus Flavius Vespasianus. Vespasian was succeeded by his eldest son (bearing the same name but known to historians as Titus) who, in turn, was succeeded by Vespasian's younger son Domitian. These three Emperors are known as the *Flavian* dynasty. Three Flavians, three short term rulers of 68-69 (Galba, Otho and Vitellius) and five Julio-Claudians were the subjects of a major surviving work of the biographer Suetonius (early 2nd century AD). Since Suetonius began his series with a biography of Julius Caesar (not an Emperor but certainly a great Roman), his biographies and the men they covered are called the *Twelve Caesars*. Coins of the Twelve Caesars form an extremely popular specialty among collectors. The portrait on our denarius of Vespasian wears a *laurel wreath* (a bit worn on this coin), a symbol reserved for the Augustus but not shown on all coins. This coin demonstrates two minor variations on the norm. The head faces *left*. Most Roman coin portraits face *right* but some periods favored the opposite view. Some issues were entirely left facing. Most 1st century Emperors issued coins looking in both directions. More unusual is the obverse legend which runs *counterclockwise* beginning at the lower right: *IMP CAESAR VESPASIANVS AVG*. The legend begins with an abbreviation for Imperator which refers to the Emperor being a military leader. While the word Imperator is the source of our word Emperor it does not equate to that title in English. Augustus means Emperor; Imperator is more like General. Most Roman Emperors made a point of claiming this military honor on at least some of their coins. The reverse is a Roman eagle with consulship date COS VI across field.

Hadrian, AE (orichalcum) *Dupondius,* 119-138 AD Following the death of Domitian, it became normal practice for childless Emperors to adopt a man of great potential and name him to be the next Emperor. In this manner, Nerva was followed by Trajan; Trajan by Hadrian; Hadrian by Antoninus Pius and Antoninus Pius by Marcus Aurelius and Lucius Verus (as co-emperors). Rome benefited greatly by this system insuring that succession would not be left to chance. This period is sometimes called that of the *Adoptive Emperors*. Our coin of this period is a Dupondius (13.1g) or bronze coin of two asses. Like sestertii, dupondii were struck from yellow brass or orichalcum. The surface of our coin bears a natural green *patina* which has been worn away from the high points of the coin to reveal the yellow metal below. Such wear could be the result of damage from cleaning the coin after it was dug from the earth or simple friction against envelopes or collectors' cabinets. Our coin also shows *pitting* or corrosion on the chest of the portrait far more severe that the porosity mentioned on the Republican page. Usually, the dupondius was distinguished by a radiate crown on the head of the Emperor. It was fashionable during the reign of Trajan and on early coins of Hadrian to use a very long obverse legend consisting of very small letters. Flat striking at the lower left destroyed part of the legend on our example: IMP CAESAR TRAIANVS HADRIANVS AVG PM TRP COS III. TRP is not followed by a numeral but should not be assumed to be indicating the first year of the reign. COS III would seem to be our best hope for dating but Hadrian assumed the consulship for the third and last time in 119 A.D. so this device could have been used any time from that date to the end of the reign in 138 A.D. An early date is suggested by the use of Hadrian's adoptive father's name in the legend. As a general rule, coins with long legends come early in reigns while the Emperor was still being introduced to the people. The reverse shows SALVS PVBLICA SC with a figure of Public Health. Perhaps this coin was issued to ward off an outbreak of the plague that tormented Rome during this period. There are literally hundreds of reverse types for coins of the adoptive period.

Antoninus Pius, AR Denarius, c. 161 AD Hadrian's successor Antoninus Pius ruled for many peaceful years and was declared to be a god upon his death. This denarius was issued by Marcus Aurelius and his fellow Augustus Lucius Verus. The deceased Emperor is shown bare headed as was the practice for *Consecration* issues. The obverse legend is simple *DIVVS ANTONINVS*, the divine Antoninus. Consecration coins used a variety of special reverses including funeral pyres and eagles carrying the emperors to heaven. This coin shows a seated Antoninus and is surrounded by DIVO PIO, to the divine Pius. Most Emperors judged 'good' by their successors were consecrated with a small issue of coins produced for the funeral. A few, including Pius, were honored by huge issues of various types honoring a ruler who was to be missed by the people. Antoninus Pius lends his name to the period of the last half of the second century. While he and his immediate successors also are known as Adoptive Emperors, they are joined by Commodus, the natural son of Marcus Aurelius, to form the *Antonine* dynasty.

Marcus Aurelius, *AV* (gold) *Aureus,* 161 A.D. This website fails to present a balanced overview of ancient coins in one major respect. There is almost no material presented on gold coins. While they exist in reasonably large numbers, these coins remain out of the price range of most collectors including this student and most of the people who have allowed him to photograph their collections for the purpose of illustrating these pages. Our exceptional example (not my coin, to be sure!) shows the standard gold denomination of the early Empire, the Aureus of 25 denarii. Only slightly larger than the silver denarius in diameter, the greater weight of gold places most aurei around 7g or twice the weight of the denarius. The coin was issued just after the death of Antoninus Pius, the time when Marcus Aurelius had first became Augustus. The reverse shows Marcus shaking hands with his co-emperor Lucius Verus promoting concord between the two men sharing power in the Empire. This time of two Augusti was a first for Rome but it was a situation that would be repeated many times over the coming centuries.

Commodus, AE Dupondius or As, 175-176 A.D. Marcus Aurelius, unlike his predecessors, had a son Commodus to whom he left the Roman world. (At this point we need to point out that the recent movie Gladiator used the names of these people but did not see fit to follow anything approaching historical fact beyond the names.) I believe our coin is a copper as (half a dupondius, 1/16 denarius etc.) but, at a weight of 10.1g, it also could be a dupondius. To know for sure we need to see the color of the metal which is hidden by the green patina. The portrait has a bare headed bust but this coin could not use the radiate crown even if it were a dupondius since, at this period, the radiate crown was reserved for the Augustus. Commodus is shown as *Caesar,* heir to the throne but not yet full Augustus. Augusti also used Caesar as part of their own titles but gave it alone to their sons or other heirs. *Bust* portraits including shoulders and clothing were always used for the lesser position of Caesar. Augusti had the option of using the bust style or the *head* portrait which stopped at the nec. The obverse legend *LAVREL COMMODVS CAES AVG FIL GERM* identifies Commodus as Caesar and son (filius) of the Augustus. Note that AVG here refers to his father of whom he is FILius not to Commod himself. He is further honored by the title Germanicus referring to recent Roman victories in Germany For which the boy was in no way responsible. The reverse shows a donative scene with Commodus seated on curule chair flanked by the personification Liberalitas and a soldier. A citizen climbs the stairs at the left and catches a coin thrown into the waiting fold of his toga (note a coin is shown just right of the citizen's head). The legend reads *LIBERALITAS AVG SC.* The coin was probably issued to be given out in such a scene in honor of Commodus being named Caesar. Commodus did not turn out to be a 'good' Emperor and his murder on the last day of 192 AD brought an end.

References

Breglia, L. — *Roman Imperial Coins, Their Art and Technique*, New York,1968

Gobl, R. — *Roman patterns for Indian coins,* , JNSI.VOL.-XXII,

Gupta, P.L. — Roman coins from A.P., A.P. Govt. Museum Series No.10, Hyderabad, 1965

Gupta, P.L.	Coins in Rome's Indian Trade, A Paper Presented at the 3rd International colloquium at Nasik, IIRNS, and Jan 8-11,1991
Khandaswamy, S.P	The Kongu and the Roman Roins, JNSI.Vol.XLVI, p.39-44
Kulkarni, P.P.	Early Roman Coins in India, JNSI.Vol.XLVI, p.37-38
Murthy, M.S.K.	Roman Coins from South India: A Study Based on Distribution and Typology. SSIC.II, p.67-76, 1992.
Narsimhamurthy, A.V.	A Roman Coins Mould from Banavasi, JNSI.Vol.XLVI, p.45-46
Sarma, I.K.	Roman Coins from Andhra Pradesh: Their Contexts, Chronology and Cultural Significance, SSIC, II, p.35-50, 1992.
Sastry, V.V.K.	Presidential Address, JNSI. Vol.LVII. p.1-13
—	Roman Gold Coins: Recent Discoveries in Andhra Pradesh, A.P. Museum Series-21, Govt. of A.P., 1992.
Shastri, A.M.	Imperial Roman Coins in Early Deccanese Inscriptions, SSIC.II, p.77-88, 1992
Sostovtzeff, M.I.	Social and Economic History of the Roman Empire, Vol.II, Oxford, 1957
Wheeler, R.E.M.	*Rome Beyond the Imperial Frontiers*, London. 1954
—	*www.vcoins.com*
—	www.geocities.com
—	www.wikipedia.org

CHAPTER-5

Kushana Dynasty and Their Coins

Kushanas were migratory people from Central Asia belonging to tribal nomadic tribe Yuechih, living in the first quarter of 2nd century BC. Kushanas are mentioned as Tokaries or Tocharian in Purana and Mahabharata. The Kushanas first occupied Bactria or Northern Afghanistan, displacing the Scythians. Gradually they moved into the Kabul Valley and seized Gandhara by crossing the Hindukush replacing the Greeks and the Parthians in these areas. Finally they set up a vast kingdom, extending their authority over the lower Indus region parts of the Gangetic valley.

The extent of the Kushana Empire

The extent of the Kushana Empire is a much debated issue. Yet, the limits may be roughly indicated, i.e. the Oxus to the Ganga from Khorasan in Central Asia to Varanasi in Uttar Pradesh. Its southern limit was marked by Sanchi in Madhya Pradesh. The Kushana capital was located in Purushapura, modern Peshawar. However, Mathura served as a second capital as indicated by a concentration of Kushana inscriptions, sculptures and coins in Mathura region.

The Kushanas in the course of their movement into India, became acquainted with the chief types of Roman coinage and those of the Hellenistic east. It is not surprising; therefore that their coinage followed to a great extent the highly developed mintage of the Graeco-Bactrians.

The initial coinage of the Kushana ruler Kujula Kadphises, follows the federal coinages of the last Greek king Hermaeus, whose conjoint issues in copper with Kujula Kadphises are historically significant. These earliest Kushana coins of Kujula Kadphises are in copper bearing the bust of Hermaeus on the obverse and Heracles on the reverse. A diademed Roman head on the obverse and figure Indo-Scythian in appearance, probably representing Kujula Kadphises himself on the reverse, are found on another copper series. The bull and a Bactrian camel depicted on yet another series of copper coins.

We have three groups of coins with the bust of Hermaeus on the obverse issued by Kadphises I.

(1) The first variety shows bust of Hermaeous to right with Greek legend "basileus Sterossu Ermaiou", which signifies Coin of king Hermaeus, the Saviour.On the reverse stands Heracles facing with Lion skin on left arm and with club in right hand. *Kharoshthi legend: Kujula Kasasa Kushana Yavugasa Dhramathidasa",* which means Kujula Kadphises the Kushana Chief or leader of the Kushanas, who is devoted to religion.

(2) The second variety again depicts bust of Hermaeus to right and a Greek legend "Kozoulou Kadphizou Koshsonou" which means coin of Kujula Kadphises, the Kushana. On the reverse is seen Heracles with the legend Kujula Kasasa Kushana Yavugasa Dhramathidasa", which means Kujula Kadphises the Kushana Chief or leader of the Kushanas, who is devoted to religion.

(3) The third variety has the Greek legend 'Baseleus Sterossu Ermaiou' meaning Coin of king Hermaeus, the Saviour.

The reverse depicts Nike (Goddess of victory) holding wreath. The Kharoshthi legend is "Maharajasa Rajarajasa Mahatasa Heramayasa" which means 'Coin of Hermaeus, the great king of kings.

Wema Kadphises was the last Kushana king who issued bilingual and bi-sciptual coins, like his predecessor Kujula Kadphises. After the Kadphises kings no Kushana monarch used Kharoshthi on their coins. They always used Greek, Kadphises II is the first Kushana king to introduce gold coinage and Roman standard along with it. His reign, it may be said, is a landmark in the history of Kushana coinage.

Kadphiese II or Wema Kadphises who established rule over India issued a large number of gold, silver and copper coins of various types. After the Kushanas the gold coinage was continued by the Guptas. It may be said that Kadphises II was actually the first introducer of gold coinage in Northern India. The main reasons behind the introduction of gold coinage by Kadphises II seems to be the demand of gold pieces for international trade going on between India, the Roman Empire and China. Through trade and commerce a fabulous amount of Roman gold flowed to India. The gold coins of Roman Emperors that poured into India appear to have been melted down and recoined by Kadphises II and his successors. The other reason seems to be extreme debasement of silver currency under Azes II and his Parthian successors, which made it impossible to continue to use the silver standard, the people having lost faith in it.

Another feature of the coinage of Kadphises II is the representation of the Indian god Siva on the reverse of his coins. Probably, Kadphises II was converted to the Saiva faith as his title Mahesvara used on coins indicates. The interesting feature of Kadphises II's coins is the representation of the king in a semi-divine figure on the obverse of his coins.

The occurrence of the Kadphises symbol and the Nandipada symbol either on the obverse or on reverse of Kadphises II's coins is another interesting feature. The gold coins of Wema Kadphises are of various varieties like the enthroned king and Siva type, king on clouds and Siva on bull, Half length figure of king and Siva type, head of king in frame and trident battle-axe type, king in Biga and Siva type, Elephant tiger and Siva type.

The copper coins of Kadphises II are of three sizes: large, middle and small. The large-size coins weigh about 260 grains and above. The middle-size coins weigh about 128 grains. The weight of the small size coins is about 60 grains. The coins of Kadphises II depict the king in various forms with different gestures and postures. The king's dresses are clearly delineated. He wears helmet. The king always wears Tartar boots, when he stands. Weapons and things other than weapons are held in the hands of the king, a club, an ankusa, a scepter. The king is represented as seated on throne, on clouds in a Biga, on an elephant and standing by the side of an altar. Sometimes only the bearded bust of the king is represented on coins. An interesting one is the representation of king as half-length figure within a square picture frame.

Siva has been used as common reverse device of Kadphises II's coins with the exception of only one type of coins where we find only a Saivite emblem "Trident-Battle-Axe". The coins of Vima Kadphises are with the imperial titles like 'Maharaja rajatiraja Mahata trata', 'Sarvalikesvara' and 'Mahisvara' etc. On Kadphises I's coin we find the appearance of the Greek deities like Herakles, Zeus and Nike, on the coins of Wema Kadphises the only deity who makes his appearance is an Indian god Siva.

The title 'Basileus Basileon Soter Megas' used on Wema Kadphises copper coins as the only legend without the addition of a name on numerous coins found all over the Punjab, as well as in Kandhahar and the Kabul valley and also as far eastward as Mathura. Some scholars are of the view that the coins belong to Wema Kadphises, while others consider it to be related to Kujula Kadphises.

Wima Kadphises' successors was Kanishka (kanishka I), who, like his predecessors, issued coins only in gold and copper; but unlike him, he preferred only one type of his portrayal-standing, dressed in a long tunic, shalwar, mantle held by double clasp at the chest and a low round cap, sacrificing at an altar and holding a spear in his left hand, but at the same time he did not confine the reverse of coins to any one particular deity. He ended the bilingual tradition of Greek and Kharoshthi and retained only Greek for a while and issued coins with the legend *Basileos Basilion Kanishkou*. On the reverse of these coins, he introduced three deities with greek name Helios, Salene and Hephaistos; but none of the figures bearing these names portrayed on coins are Greek in their iconographic forms. He soon he discarded Greek and introduced a new language – the mid-Iranian (Bactrian). From now Kanishka's coins bear the legend *Shaonano Shao Kaneshki Koshano*.

On the reverse of these coins are placed a number of deities-male and female-bearing the Iranian names-Mihira or *Mithra* (Sun), *Mao* (Moon), *Oado* (vayu, wind), *Athsho* (Fire), *Pharro* (the Iranian concept of Imperial greatness), *Nana* (nature Goddess) and *Ardoksho* (a goddess, counterpart of Indian Lakshmi). Kanishka also retained Siva of his predecessors's coins under the name *Oesho* and introduced the figure of Buddha with the legend *Boddo* or *Sakamano Boddo* (Sakyamuni Buddha).

The next ruler Huvishka introduced a new device for portraying himself. The most common type on his gold coins is that of the profile bust facing generally to the left and rarely to the right, wearing garments decked with jewels and a high or flat-topped ornamental gear, which may be distinguished into several types. He holds an imperial scepter or club in his right hand and an ankusa in the left, resting on the shoulder. His other obverse types in gold are: king mounted on an elephant holding an ankusa in the left hand and a spear in the right, a king seated cross-legged on a rock or a cloud. On the copper coins also, these devices are found. All the Iranian deities on a cushion holding a club in the right hand on the coins of Huvishka barring Orlagno. He added to the list of deities a number of new ones. Mao and Mitra are placed together on some coins which is an innovation. Huvishka's coins also have a few non-Iranian deities. Amongst the Indian gods, Huvishka has retained Siva (Oesho) on his coins and he is most common. On some coins Siva is depicted with his consort Uma (Ommo). A most strange combination of Siva with non-Indian Goddess Nana is found prominently on Huvishka's coins. also finds a place on the gold coins.

The copper coins of Huvishka are plenty. The obverse of his copper coinage depict him in various attitudes, such as riding an elephant, reclining on a couch etc. of these the former one is more common. The reverse of the coins bear like Kanishka's coins the figures of deities belonging to various pantheons, like Greek, Indian and Persian. Huvishka is almost invariably described on the obverse of his coins as 'Shaonano Shao Oeshki Koshano' i.e Shahan Shah Huvishka, the Kushana. Vasudeva is connected with Kanishka and Huvishka by the similarity of his coinage in weight, fabric and type and peculiarity consisting in the use of Greek legend only. The coins of Vasudeva are popular all over the Punjab and North-West India. The effigy of the coins of Vasudeva shows foreign influence. But his name is Indian. Though the Persian deities 'Nana' and 'Ardhoksho' make their appearance rarely on the reverse side of the coins of Vasudeva, the coins exhibit mainly the figure of Siva attended by Nandi.

He adopted the obverse device of Kanishka, i.e. a king standing in profile, sacrificing at an altar; but the king now holds a trident in place of the spear as held by Kanishka I in his left hand. The reverse devices were reduced to two deities- Nana and Oesho (Siva). Nana is seen only on a few coins but Oesho is quite common. The gold and copper coins of Vasudeva show on the obverse the usual legend: '*Shaonano Shao Bazedeo Koshano*'.

The imperial character of Kushana coinage, however declined gradually in the days of Kanishka III. His gold coins can be attributed to different parts of their empire on the basis of their types, provinces etc. gold coins of Kanishka II shows the standing figure of the king at an altar on the obverse and either enthroned Ardoksho, or Siva with bull or Nana on lion on the reverse. Coins with Ardhoksho on reverse are maily found in the Punjab area, while the coins with Siva are found from farther west. The coins of Kanishka

III displaying Nana on lion probably influenced the gold coins of Chandragupta I on the reverse of which goddess on a lion is depicted.

It is very difficult to say whether the coins bearing the legend 'Vasu' in Brahmi charcters belong to Vasudeva I or to one of his successors with the same name. but the coins with the name 'Vasu' seem to be barbarious imitations of the coins of Vasudeva I and are rudely executed.

The gold coin type of Vasu is king at altar with trident and Ardhoksho with the Brahmi legend 'Vasu' on the reverse is the enthroned goddess, facing holding cornucopia. Corrupt Greek legend 'Ardhoksho' is also found. Besides Siva and Uma, his son Kartikeya.

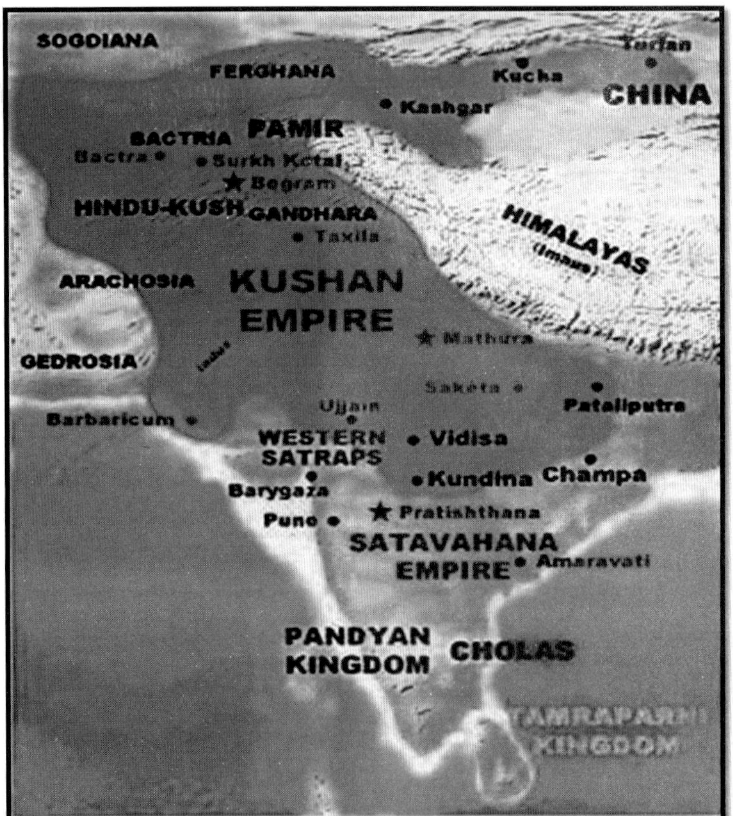

Map 6: Map of Kushana Empire

Description of Kushana Coins

The name Kushana is derived from the term Guishang, used in Chinese historical writings to describe one branch of the nomadic people, called Yuezhi or Yuechi. These nomads who were of Indo-European stock, roamed the northwestern China but during 176-160 BC, they were driven west by another group, the Xiongnu. The political disturbance in central asia (and possibly the availability of better and prosperous land and other resources) drove these nomads out into Bactria (modern (northwest Afghanistan and Tajikistan). In 165 BC, few tribes settled in Oxus valley and established independent existance. Kujula Kadphises (30-80 AD) established the Kushana dynasty in 78 AD by taking advantage of disunion in existing dynasty of Pahalava (Parthian) and Scytho-Parthians, and gradually wrested control of southern prosperous region, which is the northwest part of ancient India, traditionally known as Gandhara (now Pakistan). It was his grandson Vima Kadphises (Yen-kao-chen in Chinese record) who made Kushana a paramount power of northern India. His reign saw emergence of Kushana empire when he conquored north-western India (modern Punjab, now divided in Pakistan and India). Soon he came under influence of Hinduism (most likley embraced it for good) and took opportunity to proclaim himself Mahishwara, another name for Lord Shiva, on his coins (Shiva is a prominent Hindu god). Kushana kings introduced gold and copper coins, a large number of them have survived till today. It was the Kushana emperor, Vima Kadaphises who introduced the first gold coins of india. Kushana empire covered north west of India (includes Pakistan and modern Afganistan) and northern India. Ample evidences of trade with China, cental Asia, Egypt and Rome are available which made their economy very strong and kingdom wealthy and prosperous. Vima mostly used one deity, Shiva (Oesho in Bactrian language) standing (with trident) with (or without) his bull Nandi, on reverse of his coins. Examples of Vima's gold and copper coins are shown below.

Undoubtedly all the Kushana emperors used their coinage for the propaganda of their own superiority and the possession of superhuman abilities. The concept of showing king/ruler on the coins was non-existant in India and all the previous dynasties minted coins showing only the symbols (punchmarked coins). It was the Kushana rulers who popularised this idea which remained in use for another 2000 years. Kushana coinage were copied not only by later Indian dynasitic. Kushana coins are perhaps the best evidence we may have of this illustrious dynasty. Kushana coins tell great deal about the images of the kings as they wished to be seen by their subject. The portraits on Kushana gold/ copper coins of Vima Kadphises are amazingly individualistic, often showing him full-bearded, big-nosed, fierce looking warrior chieftain, perhaps with deformed skull, wearing high helmet, tunic, overcoat and felt boots. Shown above is very good example of his coin where Vima is seen sacrificing at an altar. On reverse, Shiva and Nandi are seen. This was the best numismatic icon ever been created in history of India. The concept of showing King on obverse and god/goddess from Hindu (rarely from Buddhist and Zorostraian) pantheon became so popular that it was used for more than 6 centuries in India on practically all the gold coins. Later, in modified form, it was used till 10th century AD. Vima like later Indo-Greek kings, also minted bilingual coins. The obverse of his coin had legends written in cursive Greek (Bactrian) while reverse showed legends in Sanskrit, written in ancient Indian script, *Kharoshti*. On reverse, the *Kharoshti* legends reads *'Maharajasa Rajadhirajasa Sarvaloka Ishwarasa Mahishwarasa, Vimma Kadaphisasha Tratara'*. The legend on reverse can be loosely translated as Emperor, the King of Kings, follower (?) of great god (god of all) Shiva, Vima Kadaphisa, the saviour. Vima was founder of Kushana monetary system, based on 8 gms of gold staters and 16 gms of copper. His wight standards were later used by Gupta emperors.

KANISHKA I

Kanishka was the son & suceessor of Vima's, who took control of this dynasty in 78 AD. Kanishka is the greatest ruler of Kushana dynasty. Around the royal head on his coins (giving himself the divine status). He and his descendents called themselves 'Devputra' which means son of god, who ruled *Aryavarta,* the India. He established an era, commonly known as Shaka era, starts from 78 AD. Shaka era is still in use in India. Kanishka's *rock inscription* has been unearthed in 1993 at Rabatak near Surkh Kotal in Afghanistan. It describes him as a ruler, his geneology and the extend of his empire. Rabatak inscription give a list of the chief cities of north India which were controlled by Kanishka. Four such cities are *Saketa, Kausambi, Pataliputra, and Champa*. This provides clear evidence that his mighty empire consisted Bactria (modern Afghanistan), part of central Asia (Tajikistan), north-western India (modern Pakistan) and Northern India till Pataliputra or Patana (modern Punjab, Jammu and Kashmir, Delhi, Uttar Pradesh and Bihar states). Kushana empire was at its peak in terms of area during his and his son's reign. Kalhan, a poet and historian of Kashmir, who wrote a famous chronicle of Kings of Kashmir, 'Rajatarangini', a crucial historic document, testified that Kashmir was part of his empire. He also built a city called Kushka in Kashmir which was named after him.

Apart from being a successful warrior, Kanishaka was certainly a man of great taste and superior knowledge. He patronized contemporary intellectuals including sage 'Shakya-muni' who had introduced him to Buddhism. Kanishka summoned a great council of contemporary scholars and philosophers to examine the Buddhist scriptures and prepare commentaries on them. A celebrated philosopher and poet Ashvaghosh who wrote *Buddha Charita*, was in his court. He built many monuments, the most celebrated of all is the great Chaitya (Shah-ji-ki-dheri stupa) at his capital Purushpur (Peshawar, which is located near the capital of modern Pakistan) which have been admired by many travellers down to late period. Chinese travellers Fa Hsien and Hsuan Tsang wrote detail description of Kanishaka's temple building activity in *Taxila* and Gandhara (modern Pakistan).

His coinage bear eloquent testimony to his zeal for Hinduism and Buddhism. Lord Shiva and bull, Nandi were commonly portrayed on his gold and copper coins, but the most important numismatic contribution of him is as follows: he was the first ruler (and perhaps only one in ancient world) who minted coins with image of Buddha. The coins depicting Buddha are extremely rare. There exist only 5 gold coins (2 dinars and 3 quarter dinars) in the world having portrait of Buddha. There are some copper coins which show Buddha which are also rare. All these coins have been minted by Kanishka, most likely to commomerate building of great stupa of Purushpur. There are two types of Buddha's coins, standing Buddha, *Gautam*, and sitting Buddha, *Maitraya*. Shown above is a very good example of Kanishka's coin portraying him sacrificing at altar on obverse, while reverse shows Buddha sitting in his *Abhaydan* pose. Also Shown above is another specimen where one can see standing Buddha on reverse of his coin. Whose shows that Huviskas was a sophisticeled rular.

HUVISHKA

Huvishka succeeded Kanishka I. The record of his reign has been unearthed at Wardak, near Kabul. Huvishka built many magnificent monuments at Mathura. He was founder of a city Hushka in Kashmir named after him (described by Kalhan in *Rajatarangini*). Kushana empire was at its zenith during Kanishka's and Huvishka's reign. Huvishka took many titles including 'Devaputra' (son of god) and perhaps was a patron of Mathura school of art. Dozens of breathtaking examples of this school of art can still be seen at Mathura museum.

His cosmopolitan outlook is amply evident in his coinage. His early coins potray him as a warrior, sporting a beard and brandishing weapon. But the transition is seen, his later coins show him a handsome king with a imperial crown and bejewelled tunic, having elephant goad/mace in his hand. This transition from a nomadic warrior to a King accustomed to court life of opulance (a specimen of this type shown above), represents the only such example in Indian numismatic history. Huvishka minted many different types of Gold and copper coins and used deities from all the three ancient religions, Greek, Zorostrian and Hinduism. Vima's coinage have dieties from only Hindu pantheon. Similarly the Kanishka's majority of coinage too have Hindu dieties. But, unlike his predessesors (and successors), Huvishka has used the large number of deities from Zorostrian and Greek pantheon, clearly suggesting Bactria was still an important region of his empire. Some of the most interesting numismatic specimen with considerable historical importance are minted by Huvishka. One such coin (which is extremely rare and highly desirable) of Huvishka shows a pair of deities, Skanda-Kumara and Vishakha. Skanda, also known by Kumara, Kumarswamy or Kartikeya, is son of Lord Shiva and considered to be god of war. Vishkha is another son of Shiva and both Skanda and Vishakha were later merged with Shiva himself. This coin of Skanda-Kumara is perhaps the earliest known depiction in existance of this very popular god. Another interesting rarity minted by Huvone is identified as god Shiva and other is his spouse Uma/Parvati (Ommo or Nana in Bactrian). Shown above is magnificent example of his gold coin where obverse shows bust of this handsome king while reverse shows lunar god, Mao with crescent at the shoulder. This is a rare coin and shows Kushana art at its height. Huvishka also minted copper coins, an example of it is also shown above. Coin depicts King riding an elephant and reverse is the moon goddess, Mao. This copper coin was very popular and was extensively imitated by the various neighboring regions during and after his reignishka show a pair of deities.

VASUDEVA

Vasudeva I took control After Huvishka's reign of this dynasty which by then had lost control over regions beyond Bactria or perhaps the Bactria itself. The Kushana dynasty had been totally assimilated in Indian culture, as reflected in his coins. All the coins were minted showing either Shiva or Laxmi. Never again deity of Greek or Zorostrian pantheon was used by Kushana rulers. Vasudeva I was the last great king of the dynasty when Kushana empire was at it's height of splendor, prosperity and opulence. Most likley, he had his capital at Mathura. He too was a patron of art and under his patronage Mathura school of art prospered. Shown above is an excellent example of his coin, which is in mint condition. On obverse is the king shown wearing helmet and in complete regalia, sacrificing at a small altar. The legends are in Kharosthi which are complete and very clear on this coin. Most of his coins were minted bearing god Shiva and his bull, Nandi on reverse. The minute details of physical appearance displayed on these gold coins while portraying Lord Shiva and his bull amply demonstrate the superb skills of die-engravers of Kushana period. Shown below is another numismatic example of this great dynasty. This is a extremely rare (possibly the only one in private collection) copper medal issued by Vasudeva. On obverse one can see bust king while reverse has a hook. It was possibly used as war medal or a status symbol.

KANISHKA II

After death of Vasudeva's Kushana empire had started its decline soon. Vasudeva was followed by his son Kanishka II who lost all the territories west of river Indus to Sassanians. Sassanians princes ruled this region and called themselves Kushanshahs and minted coins which were influenced by both Kushana and Sassanian style. Kingdom of Kanishaka II consisted of provinces east of river Indus, Taxila, Punjab and region around Mathura (northern India). His coinage can be divided into two types:(1) Goddess Ardoksho (Laxmi) on reverse minted at Mathura (2) Shiva and Nandi on reverse minted at Taxila Unlike his predecessors, Kanishaka II and kings who followed him (Vasudeva II, Vashishka, Shaka and many more) minted coins bears Bramhi characters. Shown above is fine example of Kanishaka II coin which depict king sacrificing at altar on obverse and three-headed shiva with his bull Nandi on reverse. Most early Kushana emperors minted coins depicting Shiva but coins showing *three-headed Shiva* (2, 4 or 6 armed) are shown to be minted by only Huvishka and Vasudeva I. Shown above is an example which clearly indicates that even Kanishaka II minted three-headed Shiva coins, the fact which was obviously overlooked.

After Vashishka the Kushana empire had completely disintegrated into few small kingdoms. By fourth century AD this dynasty went into total obscurity with advent of mighty Gupta emperors

Rulers of Kushana Dynasty

Hermaeus	50-30BC
Kujula Kadphises	30BC to Early first C.BC
Vima Takutu-Vima Takt(u)orTak (to) Is mentioned in the rabatak inscription. Which states that he was the fater of Vima Kadphises,and the grandfather of	

Kanishka I. He issued the coins in the name of Soter Megas.	23-45AD
Vima Kadphises,	45-78AD
Kanishka I	78-101 AD
Huvishka	106-140 AD
Vasudeva I	142/45-174/75AD
Kanishka II	177-194AD
Vasiska	199-205AD
Kanishka III	218-234AD
Vasudeva II	234-248AD
Vasudeva III	Late 3rd to Early 4th c.AD

Vima Kadphises

Wt. 14.99 gm.

Size : 2.4 (2.34) cm.

Obverse - Diademed, bearded king, seated frontally, facing left on a low couch without back rest in European fashion, feet rest on foot stool, holding a branch in his right hand, left hand placed on left thigh, wearing close fitted head-dress, a two-pronged device placed over forehead tied round the head with its end flying behind, club in the left field.

Reverse - Two-armed Siva standing, frontally, facing left in dvibhanga posture, holding trident-cum-battle-axe in right hand, left hand placed on bull, bull standing behind moving to right facing front.

Vima Kadphises

Wt. 7.95 gm.

Size : 2.06 (1.0) cm.

Obverse - Diademed, bearded bust of king, facing right emerging from the clouds, flames emanating from his left shoulder, wearing long round helmet, a device placed over forehead tied with a ribbon round the head flying behind, holding club in right hand, left hand not visible.

Reverse - Two-armed Siva ithyphallic standing in three-quarter profile facing left in abhanga posture, holding trident-cum-battle-axe in right hand and the skin of an antelope hanging down over the left arm, and also holding a water-vessel in the same hand.

Kanishka I

Wt. 1.84 gm.

Size : 1.31 cm.

Obverse - Bearded king standing to front facing left on a circular beaded mat, wearing helmet, tunic with overlapping transparent garment, trousers, holding *ankusa* in right hand and also offering at altar, grasping spear in left hand, sword hangs at left waist, scarf tied round his shoulders floating on both sides.

Reverse - Within a beaded border, Sun god with radiating nimbus, standing facing left, wearing cap, long tunic with overlapping transparent garment, extended right hand displays a peculiar two-fingered gesture, holding small standard adorned with a fillet in the left hand.

Kanishka I

Wt. 7.445 gm.

Size : 2.00 (1.9) cm.

Obverse - Bearded king standing to front facing left on a circular beaded mat, wearing close fitted cap, a two-pronged device placed over forehead tied round the head with a fillet flying behind, heavy tunic with overlapping transparent garment, trousers, holding *ankusa* in right hand and also offering at altar, grasping spear in left hand, flames emanating from right shoulder, scarf tied round his shoulders floating on both sides.

Reverse - Within a beaded border, goddess nimbate, standing to right, holding a short scepter topped by the forepart of a horse in right hand and bowl in the left, a crescent placed over the head, hair arranged behind as a bun.

Kanishka I

Wt. 7.83 gm.

Size : 2.00 cm.

Obverse - Bearded king standing to front facing left on a circular beaded mat, wearing close fitted cap, a two- pronged device placed over forehead tied round the head with a fillet flying behind, heavy tunic with overlapping transparent garment, trousers, holding ankusa in right hand and alos offering at altar, grasping spear in left hand, flames emanating from right shoulder, scarf tied round his shoulders floating on both sides.

Reverse - Within a beaded border, four-armed Siva, nimbate, standing to left, holding *damaru* in upper right hand and water-vessel pointing downwards along with an *ankusa* in lower right hand, trindent in upper left hand and antelope in the lower left, wearing dhoti in Indian fahion, a necklace of rosary beads (*rudraksha*), hair arranged at the top in *jata-juta* fashion.

Kanishka I

Wt. 7.92 gm.

Size : 2.1 cm.

Obverse - Bearded king standing to front facing left on a circular beaded mat, wearing heavy coat with overlapping transparent garment, trousers and helmet, offering at altar by right hand and spear in the left, scarf tied round his neck and a piece of its flattering in left field, a beaded rosary hanging down in the middle of his left arm, sword hangs at left waist.

Reverse - Within a beaded, border Lord Buddha standing to front with nimbus around the head and aureole around the body, wearing *sanghati*, right hand in front of the chest, holding the end of *sanghati* by left hand, wearing *ubhayansika sanghati* covering both the shoulders, headdress looks like kantopa (of present day Buddhist monk).

Huvishka

Wt. 2.00 gm.

Size : 1.3 cm.

Obverse - Bust of king facing left emerging from the clouds, wearing round helmet, a two-pronged device placed over forehead tied round the head with a twisted band flying behind, heavy sideburns, flames emanating from right shoulder, holding mace in right hand an ankusa in the left, probably wearing metal vest.

Reverse - Within a beaded border, goddess, nimbate, standing in three-quarter profile facing right, wearing loose robe, cap, hair arranged behind as a bun, holding short scepter topped by the forepart of a horse in right hand and a bowl in the left, sword hangs at left waist.

Huvishka

Wt. 7.82 gm.

Size : 2.00 (1.9) cm.

Obverse - Diademed and nimbate bust of king facing right emerging from the clouds, wearing peaked helmet with car flap studded with dots, fully armored king holding mace in right hand and spear adorned with a fillet in the left.

Reverse - Within a beaded border, goddess standing in three-quarter profile facing right, hair arranged behind as a bun, wearing loose robe, holding small spear topped with the forepart of a horse in right hand and a bowl in the left.

Huvishka

Wt. 7.92 gm.

Size : 2.09 (2.01) cm.

Obverse - Diademed and nimbate bust of king facing left emerging from the clouds, wearing peaked helmet with earflap studded with dots, fillet tied behind, fully armored king holding mace in right hand and spear adorned with a fillet in the left.

Reverse - Within a beaded border, goddess standing in three-quarter profile facing left, holding cornucopia with both the hands, hair arranged behind as a bun, wearing loose robe.

Huvishka

Wt. 7.93 gm.

Size : 2.05 (2.01) cm.

Obverse - Diademed and nimbate bust of king facing right emerging from the clouds, wearing peaked helmet with earflap studded with dots, fully armoured king holding mace in right hand and spear adorned with a fillet in the left.

Reverse - Within a beaded border, goddess standing in three-quarter profile facing right, holding cornucopia with both hands, hair arranged behind as a bun, wearing loose robe.

Huvishka

Wt. 7.81 gm.

Size : 2.00 (1.91) cm.

Obverse - Bust of king facing left emerging from the clouds, wearing round helmet, a two-pronged device placed over forehead tied round the head with its end flying behind, heavy sideburns, flames emanating from right shoulder, holding mace in right hand an *ankusa* in the left, probably wearing metal vest.

Reverse - Within a beaded border, four armed Siva, nimbate, standing frontally facing left, holding *damaru* in upper right hand, water-vessel pointing downwards in the lower right, trident in upper left hand and antelope in the lower left, wearing *dhoti* extended upto knee in Indian fashion.

Huvishka

Wt. 7.85 gm.

Size : 1.09 cm.

Obverse - Diademed and nimbate bust of king facing left emerging from the clouds, wearing peaked helmet with earflap studded with dots, fully armoured king holding mace in right hand and spear adorned with a fillet in the left.

Reverse - Within a beaded border, goddess standing in three-quarter profile facing left, wearing long loose robe, hair arranged behind as a bun, holding wreath in extended right hand and small standard in the left resting over shoulder.

Vasudeva I

Wt. 8.065 gm.

Size : 2.15 (2.1) cm.

Obverse - Diademed and nimbate king standing to front facing left on a piece of a beaded mat, fully armoured king wearing helmet with earflap studded with dots, offering at altar by right hand and grasping triedent in the left, an ankusa like object placed behind shoulder can be seen between head and trident, a sword hangs at left waist.

Reverse - Within a beaded border, three headed Siva standing to front in dvibhanga posture, holding noose in half upraised right hand and trident in the left, wearing dhoti in Indian fashion with schematic folds, hair arranged at top in *jata-juta* fashion, bull standing behind moving to left with its head stoop down.

Kanishka III

Wt. 7.795 gm.

Size : 2.1 cm.

Obverse - Diademed and nimbate king standing to front facing left on a piece of a beaded mat, wearing royal coat and trousers, peaked helmet sudded with dots, bushy hair arranged behind in Parthian style, a round device placed over forehead tied round the head with its end flying behind, offering at altar by right hand and grasping royal standard in the left, a trident adorned with a fillet placed behind the altar, Brahmi letter 'vi' in right field and 'ha' between altar and leg.

Reverse - Within a beaded border, nimbate, seated to front on a high backed throne, feet rest on a circular mat, wearing long robe, a three pronged device placed overhead, head-dress indicated by dots, holding cornucopia in left hand and noose in extended right hand, Brahma letter 'pu' over the throne on right.

References

Banerjea, J.N. — *The Development of Hindu Iconography*, Calcutta, (3rd ed.) Delhi,1974

Basham A.L. — (editor*) Paper on the Date of Kanishka, Leiden.* 1968

Chakrabortty, S.K. — *Indian Numismatics: From the Earliest Times to the Rise of the Imperial Guptas*: Bharatiya Kala Prakashan,2004

Chattopadhyay, B. — The Age of the Kushanas- *A Numismatic Study,* Calcutta,1967

Gupta,P.L. and Kulashreshtha, S. — *Kusana Coins and History* : D K Printworld, Reprint,2004

Jayaswal, K.P. — The Statue of Wema Kadphises and the Kushana Chronology," JBORS, Vol.VI, pp. 6-12.

Joshi, N.P. — *Mathura Sculptures*, Mathura,1966

MacDowall, D.W. — The Weight Standard of the Gold and Copper Coinages of the Kushana Dynasty from Vima Kadphises to Vsudeva, *JNSI*, Vol.XXII, pp. 63-74.

Maity, S.K. — The Gold Coins of the Kushana, the Kushāna Chiefs and the Sassanian Gold Coins from the Indian Museum, Calcutta, *JNSI*, Vol.XXI, pt. II, pp. 162-71.

Mitterwallner, G.V. — *Kusana Coins and Sculptures from Mathurä*, The Government Museum, Mathura,1986

Mukherjee, B.N. — *Kushana Silver Coinage: Indian Museum*, Reprint. 2004

— *The Kushanas and the Deccan, Calcutta, 1968*

— *Nanä on Lion- A Study in Kushana Numismatic Art,* Calcutta,1969

— *The Economic Factors in Kushāna History*, Calcutta, 1970.

— A Gold Coin of Bazeshko, *JNSI,* Vol.XXXIV, (Pt. I), pp. 31-35.

The Historical Significance of a gold Coin of Vasudeva II, *JNSI,* Vol.XXXVI, pp. 109-10.

— *Kushana Coins of the Land of the Five Rivers,* Indian Museum, Calcutta,1978

— *The Rise and Fall of Kushana Empire,* Calcutta, 1988

Prichard	The Date of Kaniskha, *JRAS*, pp. 911-913
Rosenfield, J.M.	*The Dynastic Art of the Kushans*, Berkely and Los Angeles,1967
Sharma, Savita	*Early Indian Symbols: Numismatic Evidence*, New Delhi,1990
Sharma, Savita & Tiwari,M.N.P.	Siva on Kushäna Coins', *JNSI*, Vol.XLV (PIs. I-Il), pp. 134-149.
—	Kushäna Mudraon mein Devi Devata (Hindi), *Pranjnya*, BHU, Varanasi, 33-41.
Williams, N Sims & Cribb J.	*A New Bactrian Inscription of Kanishka The Great", Silk Road Art and Archaeology* (4), The Institute of Silk Road Studies, Kamakura,1995
Wood, A. H.	*The Gold Coin Type of the Great Kushanas, Numismatic Notes and Monographs*, No. 9,1959
—	*The Gold Coin Type of the Great Kushanas, Numismatic Notes and Monographs*, No. 9.

CHAPTER-6

Satavahana Coins

The Satavahana rule lies somewhere about the middle of the 1st century BC. This period was marked by trade and commercial activities. The dynastic coins of the Satavahanas gain a new phase in his area with two metals lead & copper and silver were used attaking of Gautami Putra Satakarni and continued IInd Yagna Sri Satkarni.

Among the early rulers of the North Deccan no other dynasty has left to the posterity such varied and numerous coinage as the Satavahanas. Their coinage right from the beginning was predominantly of two metals- copper and lead. However a few silver issues were introduced from the time of Gautamiputra Satakarni and continued till Yajna Sri Satakarni. The earliest capital city of the Satavahanas seems to be Pratisthana. Some few significant excavated sites of Satavahana coins are Nevasa, Paithan (Pratisthan), Nasik, Tripuri, Brahmapuri, Chandravalli, Kondapur, Mansor, Adam, Hamlapuri and Pauni. The Jogalthambi hoard is the most significant hoard found till date for the Satavahana and Saka coins.

The Satavahana coins are purely native in character with the exception of a few portrait coins. So far as the symbols are concerned, the study of type and symbols on the Satavahana coins shows that their scope is very wide. The Satavahana sovereigns accepted such common symbols on their lead, potin and copper coins which thus linked up the cultural life of the country.

Simuka Satavahana was the first king and the founder of the dynasty. We have no coins of Simuka nor does any epigraphical evidence come down to us. He was succeeded by *Krsna* who ruled for 18 years. After Kṛsna, Satakarni I (c. 199-171 BC.) who was a powerful monarch came to power. Although a single coin type from his period is known was Nevasa datable in no case later than the beginning of the 2nd century BC. His son Siri Satavahana (c. 181-163 BC.) issued a coins whose based on earlier issues of his father Satakarni I. Besides issuing the Bull type coin of his father, he added the elephant type for the first time.

Elephant type coin of Siri Satakarni with the legend 'Satakanisa' on the obverse. The reverse depicts various symbols like the Ujjain symbol etc.

Satakarni II (c. 163 -107 BC.) was one of the most powerful rulers of the dynasty who ruled the longest period may be 56 years. As regards the coin evidence,

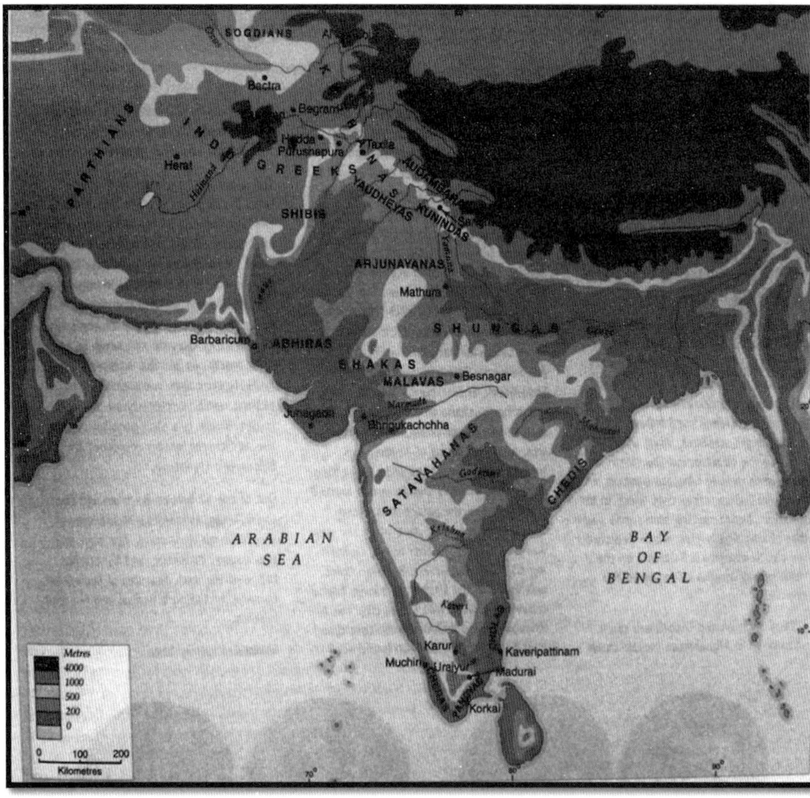

Map 7: Satavahana Dynasty Map after Upender Singh

It is not only explicit but extensive and in addition imbibed the features of the coins of the conquered territories of his home particularly those of the local rulers of Kaushambi and Ujjain. He issued a variety of coins including the Bull type, Elephant type, Three-arched type, Six-arched type, Lion type, Lakshmi type and multi symbol coins. The ubiquitous coins of his period speak of his great prowess. They are undoubtedly masterpieces among the Satavahanas issues. After him the coinage declined and became poorer in weight standard, depictions and artistic execution. The rulers following Satakarni II appear to the weaklings and the Satavahana power was dwindling. It is also quite possible that none of these rulers was politically and economically sound enough to issue fresh coinage and continued the circulation of older issues. A multi symbol type coin of Satakarni II. The Puranas refers to Apitaka (c. 107-95 BC.) after Satakarni II and assigns him 12 years of rule. We have a single coin of this ruler from Chattisgarh region, the eastern most border of the Satavahana empire. After Apitaka and before Pulumavi I we have a gap in the coin evidence for a period of about 54 years, extending from c. 95-41 BC. Pulumavi I or Patumavi appears to be the reviver of the Satavahana power, the three-arched Caitya type coins of the monarch are important.

Among the foreign chiefs occupying the northern regions the Ksaharata house appears to have built principalities in the region and its ruler Nahapana the inflicted a crushing defeat on the Satavahana ruler, possibly the father of Gautamiputra Satakarni. It took Gautamiputra a long time, say 17 long years to consolidate his power at home and then he not only re-struck the silver coinage of Nahapana but did not spare even his copper issues. Gautamiputra issued copper as well as silver coins. He issued Elephant type, Caitya Type, Horse type coins. The legend on the Gautamiputra Satakarni's coin read as 'Rano Gotamiputasa Siri Satakanisa in Prakrit on the obverse of the coin with some symbol or device depicted on it.

It Satavahana kings to introduce the royal bust on their silver issues though it is a foreign impact, the Satavahana coins are distinct by themselves in many ways from their Western Indian prototypes and depict the indigenous element in them. The Satavahana silver coins do not betray any signs of slavish copying of Western Kshatratpa prototypes, even though they adopt their general convention in the matter of weight standard, fabric, device and bilingualism. The artists of the Satavahana mints introduced in their issues an amount of originality never before witnessed in Indian coins.

Contemporary the Satavahana issued uniform type, portrait coins in white metal with bilingual legends and continued without any change in type upto three generations. Together with these similarities we see that the royal bust is purely in Indian tradition style and the customary metronymics were used unlike the patronymics of the Kardamakas. While the Saka Ksatrapas used the Kharoshthi and the Brahmi legends on their coins indicating the place of their origin and rule respectively together with that of their masters in the Greek, the Satavahanas used Prakrit legend in the Brahmi characters and Dravidian legend in the Southern variety of Brahmi characters indicating their place of rule and origin respectively. The royal busts are of special significance. They are the earliest reliable contemporary portraits giving an idea of the physical features of the Satavahana rulers who appear to be strong and sturdy with a look of determination and action.

The legend on the Gautamiputra Satakarni's coin read as 'Rano Gotamiputasa Siri Satakanisa in Prakrit on the obverse of the coin with some symbol or device depicted on it. Vasisthiputra Pulumavi II after the death of Gautamiputra by about 88 AD., succeeded to the throne. Pulumavi was undoubtedly a ruler of great capabilities and looked to the larger interest of the Satavahana empire which saw an economic prosperity under him. Sea trade appears to have gained significance as revealed by his ship type coins. Vasisthiputra Satakarni succeeded to his elden brother by force of circumstances. He continued to issue all the coin types of his brother including the rare silver portrait currency. After him many rulers like Sivasri Pulumavi, Sivaskanda Satakarni, Vijaya Satakarni, Candra Satakarni, Pulumavi IV came to power but their coins are not of much significance and are rare. They issued a variety of coins depicted symbols like Elephant, Horse, Caitya, Lion, Ship and six arched hill with named as Elephant type, Horse type, Lion type ship & Arched hill type.

Gautamiputra Yajna Sri Satakarni also issued the Portrait type silver coins. We see a sort of development towards fineness in the depiction of the royal bust on the coins Pulumavi to Yajna Satakarni. The workmanship is crisp and clean manner, brings out all parts of the bust and outline clearly into relief.

Inscribed punch marked coins of Satavahana with thin and broad flan issued in the Vidisa region (Central India) suggests that they followed the typology of the earlier local coinage. The entire dynastic history of Satavahana is reconstructed mostly on the basis of their coins. An uninscribed local coin of Vidisha depicting various symbols like tree in railing, fish in pond etc.

Coins of Satavahanas

(i) Coins of Simuka Satavahana

Metal : Copper

size : 16mm

Obv.: An elephant facing to its right with trunk upraised; a triangle ṣ headed standard above the animal, above it legend in Brahmi : *(Si)ri Chhimuka Sata (Va).*

Rev.: Part of the Ujjain symbol with double concentric circles and crescent above it; at least four swastikas as visible.

(ii) Coins of King Satvahana

Metal : Lead

Weight & Size : 168 grains, 24.5mm

Obv. : A bull facing to its left; above the animal a three arched chaitya, of which the arches are un-connected with an another; marginal legend: *satvahan*

Rev. : On the left a five – branched tree in railing; to its left a triangle – headed standard, below it probably a Tirana symbol, above the free a tarine symbol below the railing fished and river motif.

(iii) Coins of King Satakarni (I)

(a) Metal : Lead

Weight & Size : 310 grains, 25mm

Obv. : Lakshmi standing on lotus, flanked by two elephants which are shown as sprinkling water on her with their uplifted trunks; Brahmi legend in the margin : *Siri Satakanisa.*

Rev. : A tree in railing

(b) Metal : Silver

Weight : 108 grains

Obv. : Legend beginning at X, *rano siri Sata* (Ka); below it the legend, *Naganikayain* an oblong enclosure; on the left figure of a horse (or lions) facing to itself (the head of animal is off the flan, but the body is quite dear).

Rev. : Ujjain symbol with a swastika in each orb; pellet between the orbs of the symbol.

(iv) Coin of Apilaka

Metal : Copper

Weight & Size : 65 grains, 25mm

Obv. : An elephant standing to its left with trunk hanging; in front of it elephant good; legend: *rayo siva sirisa = Apilakasa.*

Rev. : Blank

(v) Coins of King Sata

Metal : Lead

Weight & size : 101 grains, 30 mm

Obv. : An elephant facing to its left; below, symbolical representation of river with three fishes legend read as: *rano sarasatasa*

Rev.: Defaced

(vi) Coin of Sundara Satakarni

Metal : Copper

Weight & size : 27 grains, 16 x 14 mm

Obv. : A humped bull facing to its left below its legs legend: *Satakanisa.*

Rev. : A tree with thick and broad leaves.

(vii) Coins of Gautmiputra Satakarni

(a) Metal : Lead

Weight & size : 51.5 grains,17.27 mm

Obv. : An elephant standing and facing to its right, truck hanging down; legend: *rario siri sataka (nisa)*

Rev. : Ujjain symbol, each ovb. of which is represented by a thick pellet with a thick surrounding circle.

(b) Metal : Potin

Weight & size : 83 grains,19.05mm

Obv. : A lion springing to itself; above it a swastika, square border of dots; legend: *Satakani or nasa.*

Rev. : On the left the Ujjain symbol surmounted by the nandipada, not very distinct; on the right a tree in railing; square border of dots.

(c) Metal : Silver

Weight & size : 30 grains, 18 mm

Obv. : In the center six-arched hill and below it a wavy line; circular legend - *Gotamapatasa sara Satakanasa*.

Rev. : In a dotted round circle Ujjain symbol with a pellet in each orb.

(viii) Coins of Vasishtiputra Pulumavi

(a) Metal : Lead

Weight & Size : 33.5 grains, 18 mm

Obv. : An elephant with jeweled neck facing to its left; trunk not visible; legend: *raho Pulumavi*.

Rev. : Ujjain symbol with pellet in each of its orbs

(b) Metal : Silver

Weight & size : 28 grains, 16.5 mm

Obv. : Bust of the king facing to his left; frizzled hair with a diadem placed round the head and the legend: *Rano Vasithipatasa Sara Pulumavisa*.

Rev. : A crescented six arched Chaitya on the right; the Ujjain symbol surmounted by a creascent on the left; a rayed sun in between the two crescents; a wavy line below; legend: arahanasa.

(ix) Coin of Vasishthiputra Siva Sri Pulumavi

Metal : Silver

Weight : Unknown

Obv. : Bust of the king facing to his left; legend *Vasethiputasa Siva siri pulu*.

Rev. : On the right a crescented six arched chaitya; on the left creascented Ujjain symbol; in between the two creascents a rayed sun; a wavy line below.

(x) Coin of Vasishthiputra Siva Skauda Satakarni

Metal : Potin

Weight & size : 50 grains – 42 grains,19.5 mm – 16.51 mm

Obv. : An elephant facing to its left with trunk upanisad legend : *rano or rana siri thada Satakanisa*.

Rev. : Ujjain symbol each orb of which contains a pellet.

(xi) Coin of Goutamiputra Yajna Satakarni

Metal : Lead

Weight & size : 121 grains, 20 mm

Obv. : Two masts ship with fish and conch indicating the sea below; legend at: *Samisa........Siri Yana*.

References

Ahmad, N. The Reverse Legend of the Bust Types Silver Coins of the Satavahanas: A Review. JNSI. Vol.LVII, p.78-90

— Some Alleged Coins of King Satavahana. JNSI. Vol.XXXII, p.58

Altekar, A.S. Some Interesting Satavahana Coins, JNSI. Vol. IV, p.25-28

— A New Silver Coin of Gautamiputra Yajna Satakarni. JNSI. Vol.XII, p.126-133

— A New Coin Type of Vasistiputra. JNSI. XIV. p.17

Angal, D.G. Early Satavahana and Other Issues. JNSI. Vol.LV, p.54-57

— Some New Satavahana Coins. JNSI. Vol.LVII, p.26-28

Bajpai, K.D. Numismatic Evidence on the Extension of Satavahana Rule in Central India. JNSI. Vol.XLIII, I., p. 63-66

Cunningham, A. Coins of Ancient India. London, 1891

Deo, S.B. New Coins of King Satavahana, JNSI. Vol.XXII, p.138

Dutta, M. A Study of Satavahana Coinage. New Delhi, 1990

Gupta, P.L. A Note on Some Published Satavahana Coins. JNSI. Vol.XV, p.187

Handa, D. and Gupta, M.K. Two Interesting Coins of Satakarni and Nahapana, N.D., Vol.XXI-XXII. p.13-20

Mangalam, S.J. and Angal, D.G. Different Varieties of Counter-Struck Coins of Gautamiputra Satakarni. JNSI. Vol.LVII, p.75-77.

Mirashi, V.V. Identification of King Satavahana of the Coins, JNSI. Vol.XVI. p.205, 1954 Note on Saka-Satavahana Coins. JNSI. Vol.XXIII, p.113

Rao, M.R. Two New Satavahana Coins, JNSI. Vol.XV, p.74

— Some More Satavahana Coins. JNSI. Vol.XVIII, p.218

Sankalia, H.D. A New Type of Satavahana Coin from Nasik, JNSI. Vol.XIV, p.54

Sarma, I.K. Coinage of Satavahana Empire, Delhi, 1980

Sastry, P.V.P. Satavahana Epoch: A New Light, Hyderabad, 1994

Smith, V.A. Catalogue of Coins in the Indian Museum Calcutta. Vol.I. Reprint. 1972.

CHAPTER-7

Gupta Coins

Gupta age is considered to have been one of the most creative phase of Indian history. They founded the second major kingdom after that of Mauryas and began to rule in eastern India in about the second half of the 3rd century A.D. It rose to prominence in 319 A.D. and included parts of eastern, northern , western and central India and continued to rule to about middle of the 6th century A.D.(578 A.D) The first two kings of the dynasty had used the title *Maharaj Dhiraj*. This indicates that Chandragupta I was more virtuous and powerful than the two early kings of the dynasty.

Gupta period is often described as the Classical or Golden age i.e. a formative period in which the Hindu social structure, religious institutions, concept of Dharma, ideas of law and polity and also canons of art and architecture came to be evolved. This period marks a major shift in the economy due to a general decline in long distance trade and the introduction of the land grant economy, the major concern being the extension of agriculture.

Demand for medium of exchange for facilitating at least relatively bigger transactions and knowledge of variegated coinage of the preceding empire of the Kushanas should have together with other factors, inspired the Guptas to issue numerous types of coins in various metals for eg. Gold , silver, copper, and lead for striking coins. The art of coinage of Gupta period was also of a very high quality. As this age was the age of Plenty and prosperity. The metal statues of the Gupta period are testimony to the fact that the craftsmen of this period has sufficient knowledge regarding metals. The talented artists of the Gupta empire had a rich sculptural heritage, financial support for producing works of art. Gupta emperors as patrons of art had employed one of the best available sculptors as die cutters at the royal mint. Traces of double striking on blurred faces of some gold coins and the appearance of two distinct devices in low relief on two sides of a large number of Gupta coins indicate that they were struck from two intagliated dies used simultaneously.

Hoards of Gupta coins mostly gold, have been found in Eastern Uttar Pradesh, Bihar and Bengal , Punjab, Rajasthan and Madhya Pradesh. The biggest of these hoards were discovered at Hullanpura village in Bayana, Rajasthan. Consisting of 1821 coins, it was probably buried at the time of Huna Invasion around the beginning of the reign of Skandagupta (455-467 A.D.)

The Gupta gold coinage shows a gradual indigenization of the currency, in its fabric, execution and Aesthetic contents. Their gold coinage was based on the weight standard of Kushans, however fluctuations in weight standard either a debasement or increase in weight is observed probably due to economic needs or a short supply of gold and a depletion of resource resulting from Huna invasions.

Chandragupta I (c. 319-345 A.D.) was son and successor of Ghatotkacha who contracted a matrimonial alliance with the Lichchhavis who enjoyed a much greater prestige. The nature of the alliance was that Ghatotkachas son Maharajadhiraja-Sri-Chandragupta I , got married to a Lichchhavi princess Kumaradevi. Consequently, the prestige, power and position of the Guptas increased manifolds and gradually a small kingdom evolved into a mighty empire. Chandragupta I was the first one to start gold coins known as *Dinars* and the innovation of incising metrical legends on coins is also to be ascribed to him.

In depth examination of the Gupta gold coins in the Indian Museum, Calcutta and the British Museum, London, reveal that a high standard of purity of metal was maintained in coins struck up to the region of Kumaragupta I. A fairly high standard of purity of metal can be detected in gold pieces struck up to a period of the reign of Narsimhagupta Baladitya. The inscriptions on the Gupta coins are in classical Sanskrit and in Brahmi script. The issuers name is invariably found on the obverse, the characters arranged vertically except on the Asvamedha, lyrist and a few more varieties are arranged clockwise. The vertical arrangement which survived till the end of the dynasty can be traced back through the later Kushana coinage to Chinese influence in Central Asia.

Among the early Gupta issues, one of the most significant is Chandragupta I's commemorative coin of the "King and Queen Type". It records the important event of the marriage of Chandragupta I with the Lichchhavi princess Kumaradevi, This coin shows on the obverse the king offering a ring to the queen and on the reverse Goddess Ambika or Durga seated on a lion with a noose in the right hand and the cornucopia (horn of plenty) in the left. After the demise of Chandragupta I came Kacha(c.325-330 A.D) a peculiar character among the imperial Guptas. Some scholors take it as derived from Ghatotkacha, *Kachasya ayam kachah*, meaning thereby "son of Kacha" i.e brother of Chandragupta I and uncle of Samudragupta.

There are no inscriptional evidence of Kacha ,but his gold coins as many as thirty which have to come to light are enough to acknowledge him among the Gupta rulers. Samudragupta succeeded his father Chandragupta I. He took pride in being a *Lichchhavidauhitra*, 'son of the daughter of a man belonging to the Lichchhavi family or

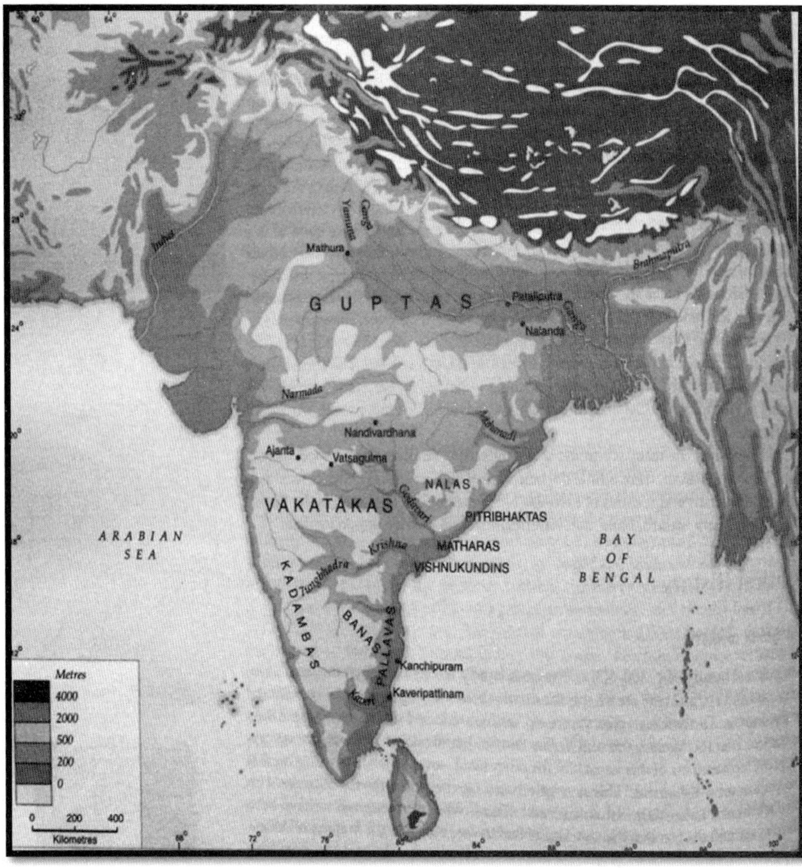

Map 8: Map of Gupta Dynasty After Upender Singh

clan'. He issued gold coins in six different type namely Standard, Archer, Battleaxe, Tiger Slayer, Lyrist and Asvamedha types. Asvamedha coins mark another important political event i.e. the conclusion of his victorious campains with the celebration of the Asvamedha sacrifice .They bear on the obverse the sacrificial horse before an altar with a legend and on the reverse the figure of the queen, who played an important part in the sacrifice. The word *parakrama* in the legend on the reverse reading *Asvamedhaparakramah*, being the exclusive epithet of Samudragupta. The metrical legend on the obverse of the coin reads "Rajadhiraja prithivim-avita divam jayaty-arhita-vajimedhah, i.e "the overlord of kings, having protected the earth, is conquering the heaven through the Asvamedha sacrifice which he has performed. Because of the Allahabad Stone Pillar inscription of Samudragupta, we know much more about him, his conquests and personal qualities. Samudragupta reigned for a long period of forty years or so, this is supported by the numismatic evidences.

Ramagupta was a son of Samudragupta, was an elder brother of Chandragupta II, and was insulted by a Saka ruler in war. He had agreed to surrender his queen Dhruvadevi to the Saka adversary.

Ramaguptas younger brother, Chandragupta II resented and devised a plot in which he disguised himself as Dhruvadevi and killed the Saka adversary. This brave act on his part raised him in the estimation of the people as well as Dhruvadevi herself; and at the same time enraged Ramagupta who tried to have his younger brother killed, but in the attempt got killed himself. Dhruvadevi got married to Chandragupta II, who ascended the throne in place of Ramagupta. Few of Ramagupta's copper coins were discovered from Eran and Inscriptional evidences are from Durjanpur, Vidisha.Either a Lion or Garuda is found on the coins.

Chandragupta II (c.375-413 A.D.) was ambitious to extend the limits of his empire and was successful in doing so. His reign was considered the Golden age of the history of India. He issued various types of coins including Archer, Chhatra, Couch, Horseman, Lion ṣ Combatant, Lion ṣ Slayer and lion trampler, Chakravikrama-type. The Chakravikrama type show Vishnu holding the disc and were probably meant as *Dakshinas* to *Brahmanas* and not for circulation. His skill in playing the Lyre finds expression in a coin series called the Lyrist type. His victory over Saka is attested by the coins which he issued in silver imitating the Western Kshatrapa silver bearing dates in Gupta era starting A.D. 320, a reckoning used only on silver and base metal coins. The Saka coins of this region cease to occur around A.D 388-397, obviously replaced replaced by those of Chandragupta II. This was perhaps the beginning of the silver currency of the silver currency of the Guptas which continued till the time of Skandagupta(A.D. 455-467) and Budhagupta (A.D. 496-500).The silver coins of the Guptas are however inferior in quality compared to their gold issues. Hoards of silver coins have been discovered in the Kutch region in Gujrat, Rajasthan and a few in Uttar Pradesh and West Bengal.On his Chandragupta II used several tiltles such as Paramabhattaraka, Paramabhagavata, Maharajadhiraja and Vikramaditya , the last mentioned being most common with the 'aditya' suffix becoming regular to all gupta rulers to follow him.

Kumaragupta I (A.D.414-455) is known through an impressive series of gold coins. In addition to the usual series he introduced the swordsman, the rhinoceros Slayer, Kartikeya and Apratigha coin types which were considered numismatic marvels.The inscriptions on these coins are metrical compositions in classical Sanskrit verse as on coins of the earlier Gupta rulers. The reverse of these coins add Ganga to the rich repertoire of motifs. Again Kartikeya riding on his peacock appears for the first time on the gold coins of Kumaragupta I. This differs from the Skanda-Kumara of the Kushana Coins of the Huvishka in iconographic form, the Gupta form being more evolved.

Skandagupta (A.D.455- 467), his successor , issued on;y Archer and King and Queen types. Among the successors of Skandagupta quite a few issued gold coins which bear titles with the suffix "Aditya" such as Prakasaditya (Purugupta), Dvadasaditya (Chandragupta III) and Baladitya (Narasimhagupta). The coins are of the archer type and of a heavier weight standard. Gupta copper mintages are rare. Copper coins of Chandragupta II and Kumaragupta have been unearthed from Kumrahar and Rajgir in Bihar and Ayodhya, Kausambi and Ahichchattra in Uttar Pradesh and Sunet in Haryana.Two rulers Harigupta and Jayagupta are known only from their copper coins. Among the more important varieties of copper coins are the Chhatra, Chakra, Standing king, Bust and Legend type. The Garuda emblem is common on these coins on the name of the issuer.

The discovery of a hoard of lead coins in the Malwa region has established that Guptas issued coins in Lead. The hoard contains coins of Chandragupta II , Kumaragupta I and Skandagupta all of whom are significantly associated with the silver currency of this region, i.e. Central India. These are another instance of replacement of the Western Kshatrapa coins in Lead after the Gupta coquest of the Sakas. The Saka lead coins are similar to their bull and Chaitya type in copper, both in fabric and form. In line with the copper coins, Gupta lead coins also have the Garuda on the obverse and the king's name on the reverse, some of them with a date in the Gupta Era.

Gupta coinage influenced subsequent coinages of many local rulers like Samacharadeva and Jayagupta of Bengal (6th century A.D.).Gupta silver coins were copied by the Vardhanas of Thanesvar and the Maukharis of Kannauj (6th-7th centuty A.D).Krishnaraja of the Kalachuri family in Western India modeled his coins on those of Skandagupta. The continued influence of the Gupta coinage lasted till the end of the 8th century in the whole of North India. The last gupta ruler was Vishnugupta who issued copper coins in Bihar and Bengal till 578 A.D.

Gold Coins of Gupta Dynasty

Chandragupta Ist

Raja-Rani Type coins.

Metal - Gold

Weight & size - 117.6 grains, .85 inch

Obverse - King, usualy nimbate, standing to left wearing Coat and trousers with his right hand he is offering a present to Queen Kumar Devi facing him to right wearing *Sari*, an upper garment and ornaments. Her right hand is on waist and the left is hanging down. Legend : under king's arm, written vertically "*Chandra*" (or Chandra) and also written "*Srīkumārdevi or Kumārdevisri*.

Reverse - Within dotted border goddess, nimbate wearing a *sari* an upper garment. A necklace and a circular pearl ornaments round the fore head seated facing on lion. Legend, on right in a straight line "*Lichchhavayah*" :

Samudragupta

Standard type - *weight in grain and size in inch*

Metal - Gold

Weight and size - 116.5 grains, .9 inch

Obverse - King standing, nimbate, wearing ornaments and coat trousers. The coat is tailed and often shows several ornamental buttons. He is holding standard in left hand and offering incense with right hand on an alter at his feet, behind which there is a standard decorated with fillet and surmounted by Garuda facing. Beneath king's left arm written vertically, *'Samudra;* out side the standard Gupta on coins Circular legend: *"Samar-sata vitata vijayo jita-ripurajito divam jayati"*. The invincible (king) who had own victories in hundred battle fields and conquered the enemies, coins the heven;

Reverse - Goddess (Lakshmi?), nimbate, seated facing on throne wearing a *sari*, bodic an upper garment, a necklace ornaments and a circular pearl border ornament round the face. She hold cornucopiae in left hand; feet rest on a circular mat.

Asvamedha Type

Metal - Gold

Weight and size - 116.4 grains, .85 inch

Obverse - Uncaprisoned horse, in some cases with a strap on the neck to left before the sacrificial post (*yūpa*) adorned with a pedestal, penon flies over the horse from the Top of post, the mane of the horse is sometimes plaited, and there is string of beads and a cresent above the back in some cases. Beneath the horse is the letter *'si'*, and below also a pedestal in some rare cases. Circular legend *"Rajadhirajah, prithivimavitva (or vijitya) divam jayatyahrita-vajimedhah."*

Reverse - The crowned queen standing to left on a pearl-bardered circular mat, dressed in a *sari*, and bodice, earing necklace armlate and anklets on her person, she holds a *chouri* over her right shoulder in her right hand and towel in her left hand hanging by her side.

legend - *"Asvamedha parākramah"*

Battle-axe Type

Metal - Gold

Weight & size 114.4 grains, .9 inch

Obverse - King standing left or right nimbate, dressed as in the standard type, but usually with sword at the belt, right hand rests on the waist, left hand a *'parsu'* (battle-axe) on left or right, a dwarf attendant, standing before the king and looking up to him cresent-Topped banner between the two, with a dot with in the crescent in some cases.

Legend - *"Kritantaparaśur - Jayatyajitara-Jajetājitah."*

Reverse- Goddess Lakshmi seated on throne holding noose in right hand and a cornucopiae or lotus bud, her legs rest on a lotus. Sometimes the back of the throne is visible and sometimes not.

Legend - *"Kritantaparashuh"*

Tigar - Slayer type

Metal - Gold

Weight & size - 116.6 grains, .85 inch

Obverse - King standing to left wearing a turban, Short jacket and a close-fitting *dhoti*, necklace, ear rings and armlets on his person, he tramples on a tiger attacking him, which falls back as he shoots it with in right hand left hand stretching the bow string to the ear on left behind the tiger. Crescent - Topped standard adroned with fillet as on the Battle-axe type circular legend "*Vyaghraparakramah*" (Valiant like a tiger).

Reverse - Goddess Ganga standing on a Makara (elephant-headed fish) wearing a *'sari'*, and close fitting bodice, earing necklace armlates and anklets on her person.

Legend - "*Raja Samudraguptah*" (King Samudragupta).

Lyrist type

Lyrist type Metal - Gold

Weight & size - 112.0 grains .85 inch

Obverse - King nimbate, seated cross-legged to left wearing waist-cloth perl borderd cap (in some cases) ornaments, on a couch with high and cushioned back, playing lute *(Vina)* resting on his lap. Pedestal beneath the couch inscribed with letter *'Si'* (abbreviation of siddham?) in Legend- *'Mahārājadhirājā-Sri-Samudraguptah.* Samudragupta, overlord of kings'.

Reverse - Goddess (Lakshmi) nimbate, seated to left on a wicker stool, wearing a bodice *sari* and upper garment, necklace earring, armlets, anklets on her person noose in right hand and cornucopia in left. Legend on the left, usually separated by a line - *"Samudraguptah"*

Coins of Kacha

Metal - Gold

Weight & size - 118 grains, .79 inch

Obverse - King dressed as in the standard type of Samudragupta standing to left holding *'Chakradhvaja'* (standard surmounted by wheel) in left hand and offering incense on altar with a right hand. *Garudadhavaja* in front of king. Under the king's left arm - *'Kācha'* circular legend - *"Kācho gamavajitya divam karmabhir-uttamair-jayati"*.

Reverse - Goddess (Lakshmi) nimbate, standing to left on a circular carpet wearing *sari*. Upper garment, earring, necklace and armlet holding a flower in right hand and cornucopias in left hand on right legend *"Sarvarajochchhetta"* exterminator of all king.

Chandragupta II

Archer Type coins

Archer Type Metal - Gold

Weight & size - 118.8, grains, .78 inch

Obverse - King standing left nimbate, wearing kushana coat and trousers with an Indian close-fitting cap. Often with a pearl border, ear rings, necklace and armlets on his person. He holds bow in left hand and arrow on right. Garuda standard decorated with fillets in his front. Written in vertically Circular legend - "*Deva*" "*Sri-Mahārajādhirājā Sri Chandraguptah.*

Reverse - Within dotted border Goddess Lakshmi (?) seated on a throne and wearing a *sāri*, a bodice, an upper ornament; earring necklace armlet and a semi circular pear ornament on the fore head her feet rests on a circular mat or lotus. In her left hand, Goddess holds a cornucopiae in some cases and a lotus in others.

Legend on right - *"Srivikramah"*

Ghatotkachagupta

Metal - Gold

Weight & size - 135.5 grains, .80 inch

Obverse - King nimbate, standing left bow with string inwards in left hand and arrow in right *Garuda-dhvaja* behind the right hand legend under the left arm *Ghato*. Only illegible traces of circular legend.

Reverse - Lakshmi, nimbate seated facing on lotus with lotus of long stalk in left hand and noose in right hand symbol on left legend on right *"Kramādityah"*.

Lion-Slayer or hunter (Mrgaya) Type

Metal - Gold

Weight & size - 121 grains, .80 inch

Obverse - King standing left or right, usually shooting an arrow at a lion at point blank range, bow in his right or left hand stretching the bow-string, king is almost touching the lion but not trampling upon it. He wears waist cloth and sash. Left or bare headed in some cases and wearing an ornamental close-fitting, head dress in others in some cases he wears a coat, in others he is bare bodied.

Legand - *"Narendrachandrah prathitarano rane jayatyajeyo bhuvi simhavikramah"*.

Reverse - Goddess seated facing on lion to right, usually with a noose in outstretched right hand and facing a lotus in left symbol on left legend *"Sinhavi kramah"*.

Horseman type

Metal - Gold

Weight & size - 120 .6 grains, .7 inch

Obverse - King sometimes nimbate, riding a fully carparisoned horse to right or left; wearing *dhoti* Sash (flying behind), ear rings, armlet and Necklace without weapons in some cases, with weapons in others. Crescent on some specimens. Legend - *"Paramabhagavats - Mahārajādhirājā - Sri- Chandraguptah"* - the great devotee of vishnu, king of kings Shri Chandragupta.

Reverse - Goddess sometimes nimbate, seated to left on wicker-stool, noose in right hand and lotus in left the stalk in some cases showing leaves. Legend - *"Ajitavikramah"*

Couch type

Metal - Gold

Weight & size - 114.7 grains, 0.8 inch

Obverse - King wearing waist cloth and jewellery seated facing, but head on left on high backed couch holding flower in uplifted right hand, the left hand resting on the edge of the couch, Circular legend- *"Devasri- Māhārājadhirajasri-cha, on right ndra (gupta) Sya (vikra) Mādityasya.*

Reverse - Goddess seated on throne, her feet rest on lotus, right hand is empty and other holds a lotus. Legend on left *'Sri-Vikramah.'*

Chakravikrama type

Metal - Gold

Weight & size - 116.7 grains, .76 inch

Obverse - God *Chakrapurusha* (personification of Sudarśana - Chakra of Vishnu) is standing to right within a double-rimmed wheel, oval in shape and going round his entire person above the knees, the deity is offering three round objects to the king standing facing him, nimbate, No legend on the obverse.

Reverse - Within dotted border, Lakshmi, wearing *sāri*, a couch below the right hand and a symbol above it. Legend on right *"Chakravikrama(h)"*.

Coin type of Kumāragupta I:

Archer type

Metal - Gold

Weight & size - 124.7 grains, 0.8 inch

Obverse - King standing to left, having arrow in right hand and bow in the left. He is sometimes bare headed and sometimes wear a diadem. In some cases and a other he is beare bodied;. The bow is sometimes hold at the top with string inside and sometime at the middle with string outside. Garuda standard behind the king's right hand.

Reverse - Goddess Lakshmi seated on lotus usually with a noose in right hand and lotus in left. Legend on the right- *"Śrimahendrah"*.

Horseman type

Metal - Gold

Weight & size - 126.7 grains, 0.8 inch

Obverse - King usually, nimbate, wearing coat and trousers, riding caparisoned horse to right or left usually holding bow in the right or left hand. Sword sometimes hanging by his side in some cases he has no weapons. The saddle of the horse often shows artistic decoration.

Reverse - Lakshmi is seated on a wicker-stool to left, holding a flower or noose in right hand and a lotus in left. Legend on right *"Ajitamahendrah"*.

Swordsman type

Metal - Gold

Weight & size - 124.2 grains, 0.8 inch

Obverse - King, nimbate, standing to right, wearing head-dress with crest jewel, necklace, armlets etc.; offering incense on the alter before him by right hand left hand resting on the right hilt of the sword hanging below the waist, Garuda standard in front of the king.

Circular legend - *"Gamavajitya Sucharitaih Kumaragupto divam jayati"*.

Reverse - Goddess Lakshmi seated to front on a lotus holding a noose in right hand and lotus with a long stalk in the left resting position on waist, symbol on the left - legend- *"Sri-kumāraguptah"*.

Tiger-Slayer type

Metal - Gold

Weight & size - 127.3 grains, 0.8 inch

Obverse - King standing left wearing waist cloth, jewellery and head-dress, shooting with bow held in right hand and strung by the left tiger falls backwards on left right foot of the king is trampling on the beast crescent-topped standard with fillet on left.

Legend - *"Srimam vyaghrabalaparakramah"*.

Reverse - Goddess standing to left on crocodile, holding lotus of long stalk behind her in left hand and feeding peacock with fruits by her right hand. Legend *"Kumāragupto' dhirājā."*

Elephant-rider - Lion - Slayer type

Metal - Gold

Weight & size - 125.8 grains, .79 inch

Obverse - King bare-headed, riding a caparisoned, elephant, furiously advancing to right, raising his right hand holding a dagger in the posture of attack. Dwarf behind him, holding a *chhatra* over his head. A lion is in front of the elephant, which the latter is about to trample with left fore-leg; the lion tries to bite the right front leg of the elephant by opening its jaw. Legend - *"Kshatripu-Kumāragupto rajatrata jayati ripūn"*.

Reverse - Goddess, nimbate, wearing ear-rings, Necklace, bangles and armlets, with hair on head tied in a knot above the Neck, standing three-fourths to right on a lotus but looking to left and holding in right hand some indistinct object before a peacock looking up towards it left hand resting on waist and holding a lotus with long stalk. The goddess is wearing a *sari* and upper garment, whose ends are hanging on her either side. No symbol. Legend- *"Simhanihanta Mahendragajah"*.

The elephant of king Mahendra destroyer of lion."

Rhinoceros - slayer type

Metal - Gold

Weight & size - 127.1 grains, .75 inch

Obverse - King bare - headed with flowing frizzled locks (*alaka*) on head riding on caparisoned horse to right wearing buttoned coat and trousers. leaning forward and attacking a rhinoceros with the sword in right hand, horse raises up its head, slightly frightened. Rhinoceros standing at bay, turning back its head to attack, mouth being open. The beast is engraved realistically and beautifully. The horn on the head left eye, two ears, circular, spots on the body the tail and the four feet being all clear. Full circular legend is (Bharta) *"Khadgatrata kumargupto jayatyanisam"*.

Reverse - Within dotted border goddess Ganga. not nimbate, standing to left on an elephant-headed crocodile, holding lotus with long stalk in its trunk. Right hand of the goddess extended, forefinger pointing out at some object, not visible on the flan left, hand is hanging down by the side, empty. Hair on the head of the goddess is tied in a knot behind and wearing ear-rings, necklace and bangles. Behind the goddess a female attendant is holding in right hand a *chhatra*, without fillet her left hand is on the waist. Legend *sri mahendrakhadga,'Rhinoceros* (killed by) *sri mahendra Asvamedha*.

Aśhwamedha type

Metal - Gold

Weight & size - 124.5 grains, 0.8 inch

Obverse - Caparisoned horse standing to right before a *yūpa*. penon flies above the horse. Circular legend - *Devo Jitasatruh Kumāra (gupto dhirājā)*

Reverse - Within dotted border queen standing to left wearing *sari* and upper garment, holding *chowri* in right hand over right shoulder left hand hanging down, holding a small towel. In front of the queen is an ornamental *sūchi* with fillet hanging down.

Legend - *Śri-aśvamedhamahendra.* No symbol

King and Peacock type

Metal - Gold

Weight & size - 128.4 grains, 0.8 inch

Obverse - King standing nimbate, bare-headed, and bace bodied, with sash round his waist and falling down, wearing *sakachchcha dhoti* and jewellry and offering to the peacock, facing him a twig of graps held in right hand, left hand hangs on the hip. Legend *Jayati Svagunairguna* and ending with *"Mahendrakumarah"*. Victorious by his own merit is Mahendrakumara (a heap of merit?).

Reverse - Kartikeya, nimbate, riding a peacock, holding spear in left hand resting on his shoulder and apparently scattering something by right hand over an indistinct object before him. Peacock is perched upon a kind of platform. No symbol. Legend - *Mahendrakumarh*.

Chhatra type

Metal - Gold

Weight & size - 119.0 grains .95 inch

Obverse - King, nimbate, standing to left wearing *dhoti*, necklace and ear-ring. Torso and head bare, curly hair hanging down from the latter. Right hand of the king is extended and is offering oblations on altar which is off the flan, behind the king is dwarf with frizzled hair on the head. Standing and holding a parasol by right hand. his left hand is resting and left leg raised up. Legend incomplete *Jayata Mahata (Jayati Mahittalam)* 'The king conquers the earth'.

Reverse - Goddess, nimbate, standing to left wearing necklace and bangles, holding a noose in right hand and a lotus with a long stalk in left handing by her side. Symbol on left legend on right *"Srimahendrāditya"*.

Apratigha type

Metal - Gold

Weight & size - 123 grains, .75 inch

Obverse - A male figure standing in the centre, wearing a *dhoti*, hands folded at the waist hair tied in a knot on the head wearing a *sari* and a tight bodice *(kanchuki)* left hand on waist right hand bent up and raised in the attitude of *vitarka*. Another figure, a male, standing to right wearing a close fitting cap. Left hand holding shield in front of the torso. right hand bent up either holding *Garudhvaja* just behind the central figure or in the *vitarkamudra*. On right side, to be read from bottom to top *guptah*.

Circular Legend - *"Pratapapara"*.

Reverse - Within dotted border, goddess Lakshmi, nimbate, sitting on a full blown double petalled lotus. Crescent in the right upper corner in most cases. Legend on the right " *Apratighah*".

Lyrist type

Metal - Gold

Weight & size - 125.3 grains, .75 inch

Obverse - King, nimbate, wearing ear-rings. Necklace and armlets. Sitting on a straight-backed couch *(paryankika)*, two sides of whose back are clearly visible, right leg folded on the couch left leg over the right one and hanging below. Fingers of the king's right hand are playing over a four stringed lute placed on the lap; the left hand is over the lute, its fingers. gesticulating appreciation.

Legend- *"Mahārājadhirāja - Śri kumargupta(h)*.

Reverse Within dotted border. goddess (or queen?) with ear-rings, necklace and bangles, sitting on a couch with straight back. Right leg of goddess is folded under the couch and the left leg in hanging down in its front right hand holds a long stalk; the left hand rests on the couch. Legend *"Kumargupta"*.

King-and queen type

Metal - Gold

Weight & size - 126.7 grains. 73 inch

Obverse - King standing to right bare-headed and with frizzled hair, wearing coat, *dhoti*, ear-rings necklace, wrist-lets and armlet. The king's left hand is on the hilt of the sword at his waist and he is offering by the right hand, bent up, a bunch of flowers to the queen standing to right facing him. The queen wears. Ear rings, necklace and bangles, her right hand is on the waist and the left one is hanging down. Crescent between the king and the queen. Indistinct traces of Legend on the right.

Reverse - Goddess nimbate, seated facing, on lion couchant to right, holding a lotus in right hand bent up and leaning on the left hand resting on thigh. The goddess wears ear-rings necklace, bangles, armlets and a girdle. The folds of her *sari* are clearly visible. Dotted border all round. No symbol. Legend right *"Sri-kumarguptah"*.

Skandagupta (?)

Chhatra type

Metal - Gold

Weight & size - 130 grains, .8 inch

Obverse - King nimbate, standing to left wearing necklace, and armlets right hand extended and in the posture of offering sacrifice, but no altar is visible below left hand is on the hilt of the sword at the waist. Dwarf attendant behind, holding umbrella. Circular Legend not complete, but beginning with *Vijitavani* partly truncated.

Reverse - Standing goddess, nimbate, facing left, wearing necklace and armlets. right hand extended holding a noose. Left hand hanging down but holding a lotus with long stalk. Symbol on the left Legend on the right *"Kramadityah"*.

Skandagupta

Archer type

Metal - Gold

Weight & size - 130.2 grains, .75 inch

Obverse - Skandagupta standing left bare headed wearing coat, trousers and boots, necklace, ear-rings etc. holding bow at the top in left hand and arrow in the right hand; Garuda standard with fillet behind the right hand. Under left arm *'skanda';* circular legend from left (different in the two varieties) not fully read.

Reverse - Lakshmi, Nimbate, seated facing on lotus, holding noose in outstretched right hand and a lotus in the left resting on knee. Symbol on left Legend on right *(Śri Skandagupta) and 'Kramaditya'.*

Horseman type

Metal - Gold

Weight & size - 140.5 grains, .80 inch

Obverse - King bare-headed, ridding on horse to left not bearing any weapons, sash flowing behind; circular Legend blurred and illegible.

Reverse - Goddess seated on wicker-stool facing left holding a noose in right hand and lotus with long stalk in the left Burred symbol on left blurred legend on *right Kramadita*.

References

Agrawala, A. — *The Place of Kacha in Gupta Chronology,* JNSI.Vol.XLIII, Pt.-I, p.71-74

Agrawala, P.K. — *A Note on the Karttikeya Type,* JNSI.Vol.XXX, p.203-206

Ahmad, N. — *A Hoard of the Gupta Gold Coins from the Rajghat Excavations,* JNSI. Vol.XXXIII, Pt-II, p.120-121

Allan, J. — *Gupta Coinage, London*

— Catalogue of the Coins of the Guptas Dynasties and of Sasanka King of Gauda in the British Museum, London, 1914

Altekar, A. S — *Catalogue of the Gupta Gold Coins in the Bayana Hoard:* Reprint, First published in 1954, 363 p, 48 plates. 1992

— *The Coin Age of the Gupta Empire, Varanasi, 1957*

Bajpai, K.D. — *The Gupta Coins from Sanchi,* JNSI. Vol.XXXIV, Pt.-II, p.258-259

Banerji, R.D. — The Age of the Imperial Guptas, Varanasi, 1933

Brwon, C.J. — *Catalogue of the Coins of the Guptas, Maukharis in the Provincial Museum. Lucknow, Allahabad, 1920*

Chakrabortty, S.K. — *Indian Numismatics: From the Earliest Times to the Rise of the Imperial Guptas*: Bharatiya Kala Prakashan, 2004

Chandra, R.G. — *A New Chakra Vikrama Coin,* JNSI. Vol.XXI, Pt.-II, p.202

Chattopadhyay, S. — *Early History of Northern India, From the Fall of the Mauryas to the Death of Harsha,* c. 200 B.C.-A.D. 650, (1st ed). Calcutta,1958

Dani, A.H — *Ramagupta Problem: A New Solution* JNSI. Vol.XXVI, Pt.-I, p.11-14

Fleet, J.F. — *Corpus Inscriptionum Indicarum. Ed. Vol.III, Inscriptions of the Early Gupta Kings, London, 1888*

Ganguly, D.K. — *The Ramagupta Problem,* JNSI. Vol.XLIII, Pt.-II, p.97-113

Ghosh, A. — *A Unique Bronze Coins of Samudragupta,* JNSI. Vol.XXXIV, Pt.-II, p.223-225

Goyal, S.R. — *An Introduction to Gupta Numismatics,1994*

Lahiri, B. — *The Gupta-Type Coins of Early Medieval Period,* JNSI. Vol.XLIV, p.155-170

Maity, S.K. — *Economic Life in Northern India in the Gupta Period, Delhi, 1970*

— Early Indian Coins and Currency System, Delhi, 1970

Mukherjee, C. — *Gupta Numismatic: Art An Artistic and Iconographic Study. 1991*

Mukhopadhyay, C. — *Goddess Ganga on Gupta Coins,* JNSI. Vol.XLIV, p.148-150

Singh, J.P. — Gupta Copper Coins on Temple Medal, JNSI. Vol.XXXIV, Pt.-II, p.253-257

Singh, O.P. — A Note on Silver Coin of Chandragupta I and Kumaedevi, JNSI. Vol.XLIV, p.48-51

Verma, T.P. — Chandragupta- Kumardevi Coin Type, JNSI. Vol.XXXIII, Pt.-I, p.44-48

Bibliograpgy

Agrawal, V.S.	1965	*Indian Art*, Varanasi.
Altekar, Anant Sadashiv	1992	*Catalogue of the Gupta Gold Coins in the Bayana Hoard*: Reprint, First published in 1954, 363 p, 48 plates.
Bajpai, K.D.	nd	"Evolution of the Iconography of 'Siva", *Seminar on Bias in Indian History* (ed. Devahuti), Delhi.
———	nd	"A New Type Gold Coin of Kanishka", *JNSI*, XLIV (Pis. I-Il).
Bandyopadhyay, Samaresh	2006	Mudranusilana : *Articles of the Seminar on Coins of Bengal and North-East India : The Asiatic* Society, xii.
Banerjea, J.N.	1974	*The Development of Hindu Iconography*, Calcutta, (3rd ed.) Delhi.
———	1957	*"Coinage" A comprehensive History of India,* Vol.II, (*The Maurya and Satavāhanas,* (325 B.C.-A.D. 300), K.A. Nilakantha, Sastri (editor, Calcutta.
Basham A.L.	1968	(editor*) Paper on the Date of Kanishka, Leiden*.
Bawa L.C. and Gupta S.C., Devi Kapoori	2004	*Elementary Numismatic Studies : Coins of India* (1835-2002 A.D.) Vol.I : vi, 122
Bebevois, N.C.	1937	*A Political History of Parthia*, Chicago.
Bopearachchi, Osmund and Weerakhody, D.P.M.	1998	Origin, Evolution and Circulation of Foreign Coins in the Indian Ocean : *Proceedings of the Numismatic Workshop 'Origin and Evolution of Coins" and the International Seminar "Circulation of Foreign Coins in Sri Lanka and Ancient Sea Routes in the India* : Manohar.
Bose, Mira & Rhodes N.G. and Bose, S K	2006	*History of the Dimasa Kacharis : A Seen Through Coinage*.
Breglia, L.	1968	*Roman Imperial Coins, Their Art and Technique*, New York.

Chakrabortty, S.K.	2004	*Indian Numismatics : From the Earliest Times to the Rise of the Imperial Gupt*as: Bharatiya Kala Prakashan.
Chattopadhyay, B.	1967	The Age of the Kushanas- *A Numismatic Study* Calcutta.
———	1977	*Coins and Icons, A Study of Myths and Symbols in Indian Numismatic Art*, Calcutta.
Chattopadhyay, S.	1958	*Early History of Northern India, From the Fall of the Mauryas to the Death of Harsha,* c. 200 B.C.-A.D. 650, (1st ed). Calcutta.
Cribb, Joe	2005	*The Indian Coinage Tradition : Origins, Continuity and Change* : IIRNS Pub, pbk.
———	1980	*The Journal of the International Association of Buddhist Studies,* Vol.3, No. 2., U.S.A., pp. 79-88.
———	1981	*Gandharan Hoards of Kushano-Sasanian and late Kushana Coppers : Coin Hoards,* Vol.VI, (ed.), Lowick N.M. and Cribb, J.E., London, pp. 93-107.
———	1984	'*Kanishka's Buddha Coins*', ND, Vol.VIII (Pts. I & II), pp. 84-49.
Elliot, Walter	2005	*Coins of South India* : Bharatiya Kala Prakashan, xi, 175 p, map, figs, plates.
Frey, Albert R.	2001	*A Dictionary of Numismatics Names* : Bharatiya Kala Prakashan.
Gardner, P.	1886	*A Catalogue of Indian coins in the British Museum, The Coins of the Scythia Kings of Bactria and India in the British Museum*, London.
Göbl, R.	1984	*Müzprä gung Des Kusanreiches (System und Chronologie der Münzprägung des* Kusanreiches), Wien.
Goyal, S.R.	1995	*The Coinage of Ancient India* : Kusumanjali, xxxiv, 502 p, plates.
———	1994	*The Coinage of Ancient India: Indigenous Coins of Early India.*
———	2009	*The Coins of India* : Bharatiya Kala Prakashan, Reprint. First published in 1922.
———	1995	*The Dynastic Coins of Ancient India.*
———	1998	*Ancient Indian Numismatics* : A Historiographical Study : Kusumanjali.
———	1994	*An Introduction to Gupta Numismatics.*
Graves, R.	1960	(Intro), Larousse, *Encyclopaedia of Mythology*, London.
Gray, L.H. (ed.)	1916	*The Mythology of All Races,* Vol.VI. Boston.
Gray, Louis,	1929	'The Foundation of Iranian Religion', *Journal of the K.R. Cama, Oriental Institute*, 15.

Gupta, Parmeshwari Lal and Kulashreshtha, Sarojini 2004 *Kusana Coins and History* : D K Printworld, Reprint.

Haaff, P. Anne van't 2004 Saurashtra (c. 450-50 BC); Surasena (c. 500-350 BC) : Silver Punchmarked Coinage : *Indian Institute of Research in Numismatic Studies*, pbk, .

Hamid, H., Kak, R.C. and Chanda, R.P. 1922 *Catalogue of the Museum of Archaeology at Sanchi*, Bhopal State, and Chanda, R.P. Calcutta.

Handa, Devendra 2006 *Early Indian Coins from Sungh* : Sundeep Prakashan.

——— 2007 *Tribal Coins of Ancient India* : Aryan Books International.

——— 1991 *Numismatic Studies,* Vol.I .

——— 1992 *Numismatic Studies*, Vol.2 .

——— 1996 *Oriental Numismatic Studies*, Vol.1 : Sundeep.

——— 1999 *Oriental Numismatic Studies*, Vol.2 : Sundeep.

Hopkins, E.W. 1915 *Epic Mythology*, Strassburg.

Jash, Pranabananda 2008 *Coins and Culture of Early North India* : Pratibha Prakashan.

Jayaswal, K.P. "The Statue of Wema Kadphises and the Kushana Chronology," JBORS, Vol.VI, pp. 6-12.

Jha, Amiteshwar and Garg, Sanjay 2006 *Numismatic Digest* : Volumes 29-30 (2005-2006) (Bound in One) : IIRNS Publications, pbk.

——— 2007 *Numismatic Digest*, Vol.31 : IIRNS Pub, pbk.

Joshi, N.P. 1966 *Mathura Sculptures*, Mathura.

Know, S. 1920 *Corpus Inscription am Indicarum*, Vol.II, pt. I, Kharoshthi Inscriptions with the Exception of those of Asoka, Calcutta.

Kumar, Manmohan 2005 *Numismatic Studies*, Vol.7 : Harman, viii, 168 p, plates.

——— 2001 *Numismatic Studies,* Vol.6 : Harman.

MacDowall, D.W. 1960 'The Weight Standard of the Gold and Copper Coinages of the Kushana Dynasty from Vima Kadphises to Vsudeva", *JNSI*, Vol.XXII, pp. 63-74.

Maheshwari, K.K. 2010 *Imitations in Continuity : Tracking the Silver Coinage of Early Medieval India* : IIRNS Publications.

Maheshwari, K.K. and Rath, Biswajeet 1996 Numismatic Panorama : *Essays in the Memory of Late Shri S.M. Shukla* : Harman, xx, 364 p, illustrations.

Maity, S.K. 1958 "The Gold Contents of the Kushana, the Kushãna Chiefs and the Sassanian Gold Coins from the Indian Museum, Calcutta, *JNSI*, Vol.XXI, pt. II, pp. 162-71.

Malandra, G.H. 1981 "Transitional Style in Siva Images on Kushana gold Coins," *The American Numismatic Society,* Museum Notes, (26), pp. 195-02.

Mitra, Anup & Mitra, Mahua	2001	*Coins of Ahom Kingdom.*
Mitterwallner, G.V.	1986	*Kusana Coins and Sculptures from Mathurä*, The Government Museum, Mathura.
Mukherjee Chhanda,	1991	*Gupta Numismatic Art An Artistic and Iconographic Study.*
Mukherjee, B.N.	1993	*Coins and Currency Systems of Post-Gupta Bengal (c. AD 550-700.*
———	2004	*Kushana Silver Coinage : Indian Museum*, Reprint.
———	1967	*The Kushana Geneology, Studies in Kushana Genealogy and Chronology*, Vol.One, Calcutta.
———	1969	*Nanä on Lion- A Study in Kushana Numismatic Art,* Calcutta.
———	1969	*The Kushäna and the Deccan*, Pt. I, Kanishka I and the *Deccan (A study in the problem of Relationship)*, Calcutta.
———	1970	*The Economic Factors in Kushãna History*, Calcutta, 1970.
———	1970	*An Agrippan Source- A Study in Indo Parthian History,* Calcutta.
———	1972	*The Agrippan Source- A Study in Indo Parthian History*, Calcutta.
———	1972	*The Pãradas, A Study in their Coinage and History*, Calcutta.
———	1972	"A Gold Coin of Bazeshko", *JNSI,* Vol.XXXIV, (Pt. I), pp. 31-35.
———	1974	"The Historical Significance of a gold Coin of Vasudeva II", *JNSI*, Vol.XXXVI, pp. 109-10.
———	1976	The Disintegration of the Kushana Empire, *Deptt. of Ancient Indian History Culture and Archaeology*, BHU, Varanasi.
———	1978	*Kushana coins of the Land of the Five Rivers,* Indian Museum, Calcutta.
———	1987	"Lord Väsudeva on a coin of King Vãsudeva I", JNSI, Platinum Jubilee Session, Volume XLIX, pp. 46-47.
———	1988	*The Rise and Fall of Kushana Empire,* Calcutta.
———	1990	*The Indian Gold : An Introduction to the Cabinate of the gold coins in the Indian Museum*, Calcutta.
———	1994	"A Coin of the Masrajha Family", *JNSI*, Vol.LVI, Pts. I &. II, p. 28.
———	1995	The Great Kushãna Testament", *Indian Museum Bulletin, Calcutta.*
———	2007	*Numismatic Art of India* (2 Vols-Set) Munshiram Manoharlal.

Index

Early Coins

Plate 1: Punch-marked coin from Ashmaka Janapada

Plate 2: Punch-marked coin from Andhra Janapada

Plate 3: Punch-marked coin, from Andhra Janapada

Plate 4: Karshapana from Panchala , India

Plate 5: Punch-marked coin from Panchala Janapada

Plate 6: Punch-marked coin from Panchala Janapada

Plate 7: Silver punch-marked coin, (*ca.*550-461 BC), Magadha Kingdom

Plate 8: Silver punch-marked coin, (*ca.*461-445 BC), Magadha

Plate 9: Silver punch-marked coin, (*ca.*461-445 BC), Magadha

Plate 10: Silver punch-marked coin, (ca.445-413 BC), Magadha

Plate 11: Silver punch-marked coin, Gandhara Janapada, : 600 BC - 300 BC

Plate 12: Punch-marked Coin, Magadha, 600 BC - 321 BC

Plate 13: Silver Punch-marked Coin, Magadha

Plate 14: Silver Punch-marked Coin, Magadha

Plate 15: Silver Punch-marked Coin, Magadha

Plate 16: Silver punch-mark coin of Samprati (*ca.*216-207 BC), Mauryan Empire

Plate 17: Silver punch-mark coin of Samprati (*ca.*216-207 BC), Mauryan Empire

Plate 18: Karshapanas from Saurashtra Janapada

Tribals Coins

Plate 1: Karshapana from Malwa region, Kausambi, 3rd-2nd century BC

Plate 2: Karshapana from Malwa region, Kausambi (?), 3rd century BC

Plate 3: Extremely rare! AE karshapana from Malwa region, Kausambi (?), 3rd century BC

Plate 4: Karshapana, Kausambi or Ujjain (*ca.*150-75 BC)

Plate 5: Coin of Sivamaga, King in Kausambi, *ca.*200-300 AD

Plate 6: Karshapana, Kausambi or Ujjain (*ca.*150-75 BC)

Plate 7: karshapana (5-ratti), uninscribed early type (*ca.*232-160 BC), Kausambi, ancient India

Plate 8: Karshapana (10-ratti), "lanky bull" type (*ca.*160-120 BC), Kausambi

Plate 9: Kanishka I (the great) Copper Tetradrachm

Plate 10: Kanishka I (the great) Gold Coins

Plate 11: Kanishka I (the great) Gold Coins

Plate 12: Huvishka, Gold Coins

Plate 13: Huvishka, Gold Coins

Plate 14: Vasudeva I, Gold Coins

Plate 15: Vasudeva I, Gold Coins

Plate 16: Kanishka II, Gold Coins

Plate 17: Vashishka, Gold Coins

Satvahan Coins

Plate 1: Copper Karshapana, Early Satakarni Issue, Maharashtra - Vidarbha type 39 BC - 220 AD

Plate 2: Copper Karshapana, Early Satakarni Issue, Maharashtra - Vidarbha type 39 BC - 220 AD

Plate 3: Copper Karshapana, Early Satakarni Issue, Maharashtra - Vidarbha type, 39 BC - 220 AD

Plate 4: Copper Karshapana, Early Satakarni Issue, Maharashtra - Vidarbha type 39 BC - 220 AD

Plate 5: Copper Karshapana, Siri Satakarni (Satkarni-I), Maharashtra - Vidarbha type, 40 BC - 22 BC

Plate 6: Copper Karshapana, Siri Satakarni (Satkarni-I), Maharashtra - Vidarbha type, 40 BC - 22 BC

Plate 7: Copper Karshapana, Siri Satakarni (Satkarni-I) , Vidarbha type 40 BC - 22 BC

Plate 8: A multi symbol type coin of Satakarni II

Plate 9: Copper, Chhimuka Satavahana, Vidarbha region

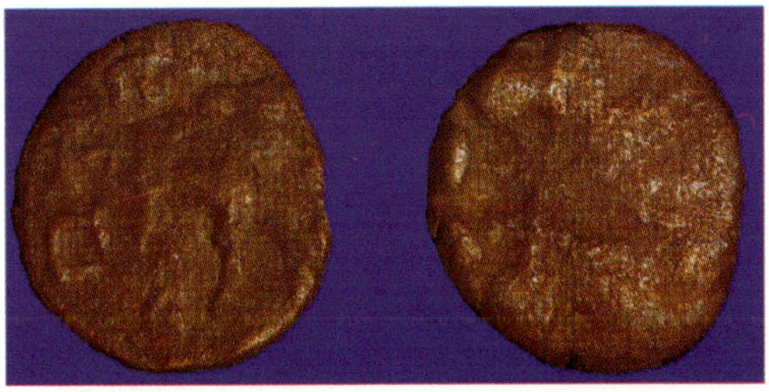

Plate 10: Satavana bronze coins (nevasa-Paithan series) counter struck by nahapana

Plate 11: Satavana bronze coins (nevasa-Paithan series) counter struck by nahapana

Plate 12: Lead coin of Gotamiputra Siva Satakarni

Plate 13: Vasithiputa Isimulas lead coin in the Junnar "Lion type"

Plate 14: Elephant type coin of Siri Satakarni

Plate 15: Restruck coins of Nahapana by Gautamiputra Satakarni

Gupta Gold Coins

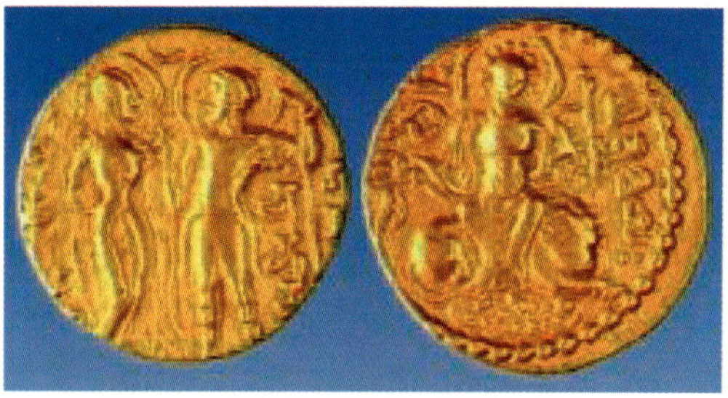

Plate 1: King-Queen Type Coins, Chandragupta I

Plate 2: King-Queen Type Coins, Chandragupta I

Plate 3: A Chakradhvaja Type gold coins of Kach Gupta

Plate 4: A Chakradhvaja Type gold coins of Kach Gupta

Plate 5: Samudragupta.Ashvamedha type Gold Coins

Plate 6: Samudragupta Ashvamedha type Gold Coins

Plate 7: A Tiger slayer type Gold coins of Samudragupta

Plate 8: A Battel axe type Gold coins of Samudragupta

Plate 9: A Battel axe type Gold coins of Samudragupta

Plate 10: A standard type Gold coins of Samudragupta

Plate 11: A Archer type Gold coins of Samudragupta

Plate 12: A Lyrist type Gold coins of Samudragupta

Plate 13: A Lyrist type Gold coins of Samudragupta

Plate 14: A tiger slayer type Gold coins of Samudragupta

Plate 15: A standard type Gold coins of Chandragupta II

Plate 16: A Archer type Gold coins of Chandragupta II

Plate 17: A Archer type Gold coin of Chandragupta II

Plate 18: A Archer type Gold coin of Chandragupta II

Plate 19: A Archer type Gold coin of Chandragupta II

Plate 20: A Archer type Gold coin of Chandragupta II

Plate 21: A Horseman type Gold coin of Chandragupta II

Plate 22: A Horseman type Gold coin of Chandragupta II

Plate 23: A Lion slayer type Gold coin of Chandragupta II

Plate 24: A Lion slayer type Gold coin of Chandragupta II

Plate 25: A Chhatra type Gold coin of Chandragupta II

Plate 26: A Chhatra type Gold coin of Chandragupta II

Plate 27: A couch type Gold coin of Chandragupta II

Plate 28: A couch type Gold coin of Kumargupta I

Plate 29: A Horseman type Gold coin of Kumargupta I

Plate 30: A Horseman type Gold coin of Kumargupta I

Plate 31: A Tiger slayer type Gold coin of Kumargupta I

Plate 32: A Tiger slayer type Gold coin of Kumargupta I

Plate 33: A Peacock (Kartikeya) type Gold coin of Kumargupta I

Plate 34: A Peacock (Kartikeya) type Gold coin of Kumargupta I

Plate 35: A Peacock (Kartikeya) type Gold coin of Kumargupta I, N.M. collection

Plate 36: A Apratigha type Gold coin of Kumargupta I, BKB collection

Plate 37: A Archer type Gold coin of Kumargupta I

Plate 38: A King-Queen type Gold coin of Kumargupta I

Plate 39: A Archer type Gold coin of Kumargupta II

Plate 40: A Archer type Gold coin of Kumargupta II

Plate 41: A Archer type Gold coin of Budhagupta

Plate 42: A Horseman Lion slayes type Gold coin of Budhagupta

Plate 43: A Archer type Gold coin of Chandragupta III

Plate 44: A Archer type Gold coin of Chandragupta III

Plate 45: A Archer type Gold coin of Chandragupta III

Plate 46: A Archer type Gold coin of Narasimhagupta

Plate 47: A Archer type Gold coin of Narasimhagupta

Plate 48: A Archer type Gold coin of Vishnugupta

Plate 49: A Archer type Gold coin of Puragupta (or Purugupta)

Plate 50: A Archer type Gold coin of Puragupta (or Purugupta)